THE TRUST PROBLEM

THE TRUST PROBLEM

BY

EDWARD DANA DURAND, Ph.D.

PROFESSOR OF STATISTICS IN THE UNIVERSITY
OF MINNESOTA, RECENTLY DIRECTOR OF
THE UNITED STATES CENSUS

CAMBRIDGE
HARVARD UNIVERSITY PRESS
LONDON: HUMPHREY MILFORD
Oxford University Press
1915

REPRINTED FROM THE
QUARTERLY JOURNAL OF ECONOMICS

CONTENTS

THE TRUST PROBLEM

THE TRUST PROBLEM

CHAPTER I

THE NECESSITY OF PROHIBITION OR REGULATION

IN these lectures, we shall confine ourselves to the consideration of trusts and pools, without attempting to cover the whole field of monopoly or of contracts in restraint of trade. The term trust will be used to describe the closely-knit combination or consolidation. The most familiar forms are three: first, the combination through the holding of stock by trustees, once so common, but now disused; second, the holding corporation; and, third, the corporate merger, in which a single company acquires direct title to the property of the combining concerns. Most people use the term trust essentially to cover combinations of these three classes, altho sometimes it is applied to any kind of combination or any case of supposed monopoly. Under the trust, the entire business of the combining plants, including productive processes as well as marketing policy, is subject to a single control.

On the other hand, we shall use the term pool to designate any combination of previously competing plants which retain their independence with respect to the processes of production. Strictly speaking, the word pool implies division of output or of profits among the constituent concerns. For brevity, however, even at the expense of strict accuracy, it may be employed more broadly to include agreements as to prices, even where there is no division of the output. As a matter of fact, most price agreements involve a more or less definite division of business, since without it the maintenance of prices is very difficult.

It is customary to use the term "industrial combinations" as synonymous with trusts and pools. There are, however, many combinations which possess only a minor fraction of the business in which they are engaged, which have no monopolistic intent and no possibility of exercising any monopolistic power. The trusts and the pools, in the sense in which we shall use the terms, have been organized primarily in the hope of securing monopolistic control of prices. How far they have been able to realize this purpose is one of the main questions for our consideration. In some cases, for brevity, we shall use the term "combinations" to designate trusts and pools, but when doing so, we have in mind only those combinations which have taken in a large proportion of the plants in their respective industries and have aimed at monopoly.

The recent rapid growth of trusts has so focussed public attention that the importance of pools is often overlooked. The number of pools has been, and still remains, far greater than the number of trusts. They probably affect a larger volume of business. Many of the arguments as to the effects of combinations, their advantages and disadvantages, which apply to trusts, do not apply to pools.

There are at bottom only three possible ways of dealing with trusts and pools. We may seek to prevent them from competing unfairly and to deprive them of special privileges giving an advantage over competitors, but otherwise leave them alone. Practically no one, I take it, would favor the plan of not even placing restrictions upon their methods of competition or seeking to deprive them of special privileges. Second, we may permit trusts and pools to exist but regulate their prices and profits. Third, we may undertake to destroy them. The broad problem before the American people is the choice among these three policies, — *laissez faire*, regulation, and prohibition.

In my opinion, the first of these policies is inadequate. I shall attempt to show in the present lecture that it is desirable either to regulate the trusts and pools, or to destroy and prevent them as best we can. In subsequent lectures I shall consider the relative merits of regulation and prohibition.

Many believe, — economists and others, — that the trust or the pool cannot, merely by virtue of combination, maintain such monopolistic power as to injure the public. They hold that the power of such combinations, so far as it exists at all, rests mainly on unfair competitive methods or on special privileges, such as the possession of some natural or patent monopoly. They believe that in the absence of these "unfair" advantages competition, actual or potential, will serve to hold the prices charged by trusts and pools at a reasonable level. All we need is to draw the teeth of the combinations. The combination may indeed maintain excessive prices for a time. Before long, however, competitors will arise and force prices down again. Ultimately, continues the argument, the combination will either lose its controlling proportion of the business, or it will adopt the policy of maintaining prices so low that competitors will not be tempted to come into the field.

Experience lends some support to this position. Many a pool has gone to pieces in the past as the result of the attempt to maintain exorbitant prices. Not a few among the trusts have a smaller proportion of the business in their fields today than they had at the time of their organization. Others have maintained moderate prices. It is perfectly true, moreover, that the trusts which have been most powerful have been those which used unfair competitive practices or possessed natural or patent monopolies. The Standard Oil Company, for example, has almost continuously been able, throughout the greater part of the country, to extort prices far above a normal competitive level. The Standard Oil Company has probably outdone every other combination in unfair competitive practices. It has also been aided by the element of natural monopoly in pipe-line transportation and in tank-wagon delivery.

It must be conceded, then, that the power of a combination, merely as such, to maintain monopoly prices is not without limit. Competition is a restraining influence. But those who would have us keep hands off the trusts and pools must prove much more than this. They must prove that it is possible to prevent combinations from using unfair competitive methods and to deprive them of special sources of monopoly power. They must prove that, if this is accomplished, the combinations will possess practically *no* monopoly power whatever, that on the average and in the long run they can maintain prices *no* higher than would prevail if combinations were destroyed. The fact that competition will bring down prices next year to a reasonable level is not sufficient comfort for the consumers who are paying exorbitant prices this year. The fact that a trust in one industry charges reasonable prices in order to ward off competition will not quiet the complaints of the consumers of the products of another combination which adopts the opposite policy.

There can be no conclusive generalization from experience regarding the effect of combinations upon prices, still less regarding the ability of combinations to maintain monopoly prices in the absence of unfair competition and special privileges. For this there are several reasons.

In the first place, there has been no complete investigation of the multitude of trusts and pools. The thoro investigations of the Bureau of Corporations have covered only a half dozen industries. Other less elaborate investigations, official or private, have been made, but the results of most of them are inconclusive. Many fields have not been touched at all.

In the second place, law and public opinion have had an important effect in restraining the monopoly power of trusts and pools. Up to about fifteen years ago, there were very few trusts. The pool was the common form of combination. Even before the enactment of the Sherman law in 1890, and of the various state anti-trust acts, most of which were passed at about that date, pooling agreements were void and unenforceable under the common law. There was nothing to prevent their members from breaking away. Since the passage of the anti-trust acts, pools have been criminal as well as unenforceable. If pooling were legalized, if pool agreements were made enforceable, the power of pools might be much greater than it has been in the past.

In any case, we cannot judge the monopoly power of the trusts from past experience with the pools. From the trust no member can possibly break away. But we have had no adequate test of the monopoly power of trusts unrestrained by law. Practically the entire history of the trusts is comprised in the period since the Sherman act was passed. They have operated under the ban of law. That fact has affected their price policies and their policies with respect to the acquisition of competitors. The effect must have been appreciable even in the earlier days, when the anti-trust laws were not being actively enforced. It has been powerful during more recent years, when suits in equity and indictments against trusts have been almost weekly events. The trusts have not dared to fight their competitors so vigorously or to annex them so freely as they would have done in the absence of restrictive legislation. They have hardly dared to maintain prices as high as they have had power to do. They have feared dissolution. They have feared criminal prosecution. They have desired to curry public favor with a view to securing amendments making the laws less rigid. What they would or could do if given free rein cannot be judged by past experience.

In the third place, a satisfactory study of the effect of trusts and pools on prices during recent years is made particularly difficult by the extraordinary changes which have taken place in industry generally. There was from 1897 until a year or two ago a long period of high prosperity, of rapidly advancing prices, and of rapid changes in methods of production, not merely in trust controlled industries, but in industries generally. It is, therefore, quite impossible in most cases to determine the effect of a trust on prices by merely comparing the prices before and after the formation of the trust. It is necessary in each case to enter into the most elaborate details as to the prices of materials, the rates of wages, the methods of production and the movements of demand.

Some have sought to measure the influence of trusts merely by comparing the movement of prices in industries in which trusts exist with that in other industries. The prices of farm products are often used for such comparison. On the average the prices of agricultural products have advanced more than those of trust-made articles. Comparisons of this sort, however, prove absolutely nothing. The disparity between the growth of population and that of agricultural production has caused an extraordinary increase in the prices of farm products. Of course other factors besides the presence or absence of combinations affect the relative price movements of individual commodities or groups of commodities. Under conditions of freest competition the price of one product may go up while that of another goes down, or the price of one may go up far faster than that of the other. The sole question at issue is whether the price of the particular commodity made by a particular trust has gone up more or has fallen less than it would have done in the absence of combination. That question, as already suggested, can be settled, if at all, only by the most elaborate investigations.

Finally, even if we possessed far more information than we do on the history of prices under trusts and pools, we should still be unable to determine satisfactorily to what extent such power as these combinations were found to possess over prices was attributable to unfair competitive methods or to special privileges such as natural or patent monopolies. Unfair competitive practices are largely secret. Railroad discriminations, for example, are comparatively seldom brought to light. We shall never know how far combinations and pools in the past have used unfair methods. Even if we did know all about these practices and all about the special privileges enjoyed by combinations, it would be merely a question of opinion as to how far power over prices was attributable to them, except in cases where no unfair practices and no special privileges had existed.

The truth is that a final answer to the question whether trusts and pools, merely by virtue of combination, can maintain monopoly power and can on the average keep prices higher than those prevailing under strictly competitive conditions, would be possible only as the result of a wide-reaching and prolonged experiment. The nation and the states would have to repeal their anti-trust laws and substitute merely laws for the prevention of unfair competitive methods and the removal of special monopoly privileges. Then, perhaps, after a long period of years, we could determine approximately the advantages or disadvantages of unrestrained liberty to combine. It is such an experiment, apparently, that some would have us undertake. The chief objection to it would be the difficulty of dropping the experiment when we had learned its lesson. If it were found that trusts and pools under such conditions were injurious to the public interests, it would be almost impossible to break them up and to return to a régime of general competition.

Are we then to reach the conclusion that we know nothing about the ability of trusts and pools to obtain excessive prices if unaided by unfair competitive methods or special advantages? Must we give up the solution of the trust problem at the outset? I think not. There is enough evidence at least to indicate the probability that combination of the greater part of the concerns in an industry, merely as such, gives an appreciable degree of monopoly power.

In the case of a good many trusts and pools we have reason to believe, either from the mere nature of their business or from the results of investigation, that unfair competitive methods and special monopolistic features have not been important factors. Yet in some such instances monopolistic prices have been maintained for greater or shorter periods of time.

Pools are much less able than trusts to use unfair competitive methods effectively. This is the natural result of the fact that the pool is not under unified management. Take the matter of railroad discriminations, for example. The pool ordinarily does not deal with the railroads as a unit. It has no officer or organization for that purpose. The individual members either pay the regular freight rates or separately negotiate for special rates and rebates. As individual concerns, the members of a pool are not in a stronger position to secure railroad favors than the outside concern. The practice of price discrimination also requires, in order to be an effective agent for destroying competition, a degree of centralization in marketing such as seldom exists in the pool.

Moreover, in most cases, the pool as such can have no peculiar monopoly privileges. Only in case the single members together possess the whole of some limited natural resource, or together possess all the patents on which a given business is dependent, can their combination have a peculiar advantage over outside concerns. It could readily be shown that, in the case of most pools, no such conditions exist.

Nevertheless, even pools have often exercised a powerful monopolistic control over prices. The successive pools in the powder business, the pools of salt manufacturers, the pools of iron and steel manufacturers, notably the wire-nail pool of the 90's, the more recent pools in certain specialized branches of the wire industry, — these and a number of others are known to have advanced prices greatly. It is not sufficient to say that in most or even in all cases the excessive prices have been only temporarily maintained. It must be shown that during the ensuing period of competition the prices were enough below the normal level to offset the monopoly prices of the preceding period. This cannot be shown; the facts, at least in a good many cases, have been otherwise. The public has been forced on the average to pay excessive prices as the result of pools. As already indicated, moreover, the breaking down of pool prices has quite as often been due to the action of the members of the pool itself as to competition from without. To show that pools cannot maintain monopoly would not be to show that trusts, with their stronger organization, cannot do so.

Turning now to our experience with trusts, it has been demonstrated by thoro investigation that several of the trusts have maintained prices, sometimes for long periods, far above the competitive level. This has been proved true of the oil, steel, sugar and tobacco trusts. Doubtless it has been true also of many others not so investigated. Of the four named the oil trust is exceptional. It has in such large measure resorted to unfair competitive methods and has possessed such special privileges as might possibly account fully for the monopoly power displayed. I do not think the same can be said of the others.

The history of the sugar trust is illuminating. While that combination has at times profited by railroad discriminations, there is little reason to believe that its ability to attack competitors was due in any great measure to such discriminations. Most of the competitors which have arisen from time to time have been exceedingly large concerns, whose business the railroads were eager enough to get. Price discrimination and other unfair methods of competition can be used in the sugar industry only within narrow limits. These methods were certainly not the means which prevailed to force competitors to sell out to the trust. For about fifteen years after the formation of the sugar trust in 1887, sugar prices, — that is, the margins between the prices of raw and refined sugars, — showed marked oscillations. A period of high monopolistic prices would be followed by the erection of new plants and a period of active competition. The competitors would then be taken into the fold and prices advanced again. On the average, prices were materially higher than they would have been under normal competition. For the past ten years or thereabouts, conditions in the trade have been more steady and margins have varied but little, being on the whole rather high. The trust has lost materially in its control of output during that period. The fact, however, seems to me attributable more to the fear of government prosecution than to a change of heart on the part of the managers of the combination or to realization of their inability to maintain monopoly.

The tobacco trust possessed for a long time, if it does not still possess, very great monopolistic power. When the Spanish war broke out, the government greatly increased the taxes on tobacco. Manufacturers, as was expected, advanced the prices correspondingly. At the close of the war, the taxes were restored to their former level. But prices were not reduced. Profits soared. Had effective competition existed in the trade, it would have been impossible to maintain prices after the taxes were lowered. The tobacco trust, I feel sure, was far from owing the whole of its power to unfair competitive methods or to special monopoly privileges. Freight charges on tobacco are such a small element in cost that, even if the trust had special favors in this respect, they could have counted but little in competition. The trust did make considerable use of price discrimination as a method of warfare against competitors. It maintained bogus independent companies. It sought to make exclusive contracts with dealers. The conditions of the trade, however, are such that these practices could not wholly account for monopoly power. The ability of the trust to maintain its dominant position was largely due to its readiness to buy up competitors at good prices, and to the readiness of competitors to submit to the amalgamation process.

In the case of the steel industry, the maintenance of a generally high level of prices since about 1900 has been due largely to the willingness of the principal independent concerns to follow the lead of the Steel Corporation. The understandings with outside concerns have been usually very informal, but decidedly effective. The steel combination is much bigger than the Steel Corporation. That Corporation has gradually lost in its proportion of the output, but its power over prices has scarcely diminished. Unfair practices have contributed but little to its strength.

The truth is that in by no means all industries is it possible for a combination, however comprehensive, to add much to its power by unfair competitive methods. Still fewer industries possess peculiar monopolistic factors which tend to strengthen the power resulting merely from the combination of the greater part of the industry.

The importance of railroad discriminations, for example, as a factor in the monopoly power of the trusts has often been exaggerated. Such discriminations were undoubtedly of enormous aid to the Standard Oil Trust. They have been of considerable assistance to a good many other trusts. But for not a few industries in which combinations have developed, freight charges are a relatively unimportant element of cost. During the past fifteen years, which cover the entire history of many of the trusts, railroad discriminations have been much less common than formerly. Law has done much to eliminate them. So has the increased traffic of the railroads, which has made them less eager to take business away from one another. The government investigations have failed to show that the harvester or tobacco trusts enjoyed special favors of importance from the railroads. They also have failed to show that the Steel Corporation has received such favors, other than those arising from its operation of switching railroads at its plants; and similar advantages were enjoyed by the leading independent steel concerns as well. It would be rash to say positively that this or that particular trust has had no unfair advantage over competitors in railroad rates, but it is certain that by no means every trust has had such advantage.

Again, price discrimination is not possible in all cases. True, it has been a tremendously powerful weapon in the hands of the Standard Oil Company. The peculiar method of marketing the principal petroleum products, by delivery in tank-wagons directly to the door of the retail dealer, greatly facilitated this practice. For example, some years ago the Standard Oil Company was selling illuminating oil at San Francisco, next door to its great California refinery, for 12½ cents a gallon. It was transporting the same oil several hundred miles to Los Angeles and selling it for 7½ cents. Half a cent a gallon is a fair profit on oil. The small competing refineries were located chiefly near Los Angeles. In many industries, however, price discrimination cannot be made an effective tool of monopoly. In the case of those products which are standard in character and which are handled through central markets, comparatively little can be gained by it.

So, too, the practice of requiring exclusive patronage, — refusing to sell goods at all except to those who agree to refrain from buying the goods of competitors, — can be made a means of aiding monopoly in comparatively few industries. In the case of staple goods obtainable at central markets, it makes no difference to the purchaser whose product he buys. He runs little risk that by refusing to buy from a given seller, even the principal producer, he may be unable to supply himself from other sources. Where a combination has already, by patent rights, reputation or otherwise, a practical monopoly of certain products, it can sometimes use that monopoly as a means of forcing purchasers to buy its other products also, to the exclusion of those made by competitors. Otherwise the practice of requiring exclusive patronage seldom tends to monopoly. Indeed, it is a very common practice among concerns which have neither monopoly power nor monopoly purpose.

Some of the combinations have owed a good deal of their power to the possession of natural or patent monopolies. The grip of the Standard Oil Company was greatly strengthened by the system of pipe-line transportation, which, like other means of transportation, tends strongly to monopoly. The system of tank-wagon delivery of oil to dealers also lends itself to monopoly, since duplication of service means needless expense. The possession of limited natural resources has aided at least a small number of the trusts to maintain their power. The possession of patents has been a factor of some importance in the case of the American Can Company, of the combinations in the electrical industry, in the shoe machinery industry and a few others. Were it possible to deprive trusts of these special monopolistic privileges, or to control the exercise of them by fixing transportation rates, fixing prices or rentals for patented articles or otherwise a number of the trusts would be decidedly weakened.

Nevertheless, it is far from true that factors of this sort are present in a majority of the combinations. They count little, for example, in the sugar business, or the tobacco business, or the meat-packing business. I doubt even if the United States Steel Corporations has owed any appreciable part of its power in the past to the ownership of ore lands or the operation of railroads and steamships, considered merely as elements of natural monopoly.

It would, of course, require volumes to enter into all the details of the known facts regarding the individual combinations and to discuss carefully their significance. The statements I have made thus briefly may be challenged. Some of them may not be well-founded. On the whole, however, after much observation and study, I am strongly of the opinion that past experience goes to show that trusts and pools, merely by virtue of combination, can work injury to the public, through excessive prices. I do not believe that experience supports the contention that to prohibit unfair competitive methods and to deprive combinations of special monopolistic privileges would sufficiently protect the people from extortion.

The opinion that the possession of a dominant proportion of a given business will by itself enable an industrial combination to exercise monopoly power over prices is not without theoretical support.

Some economists go so far as to maintain, on abstract grounds as well as on the ground of experience, that under modern conditions continued competition is impossible in most fields of manufacturing industry. They hold that the large amount of fixed capital places modern manufacturing industries in the same category with railroads. It has long been recognized that competition among railroads tends to go to such excessive lengths as virtually to force combination in self protection. Those who take this view would have us adopt neither the policy of permitting combinations to go unrestrained, nor the policy of attempting to destroy and prevent them. They find the only possible solution of the trust problem in government regulation of prices and profits.

This view seems to me extreme. It will be discussed more fully in another lecture. There is a material difference between the conditions in the great majority of manufacturing industries and those in railroad transportation. To maintain that it is impossible by law to prevent combinations in restraint of trade is very different from maintaining that, in the absence of laws against such combinations, they will be able to exercise a large degree of monopoly power. However, whatever force there may be in the arguments in behalf of the first of these positions is obviously still greater in behalf of the second.

Against this extreme view, that competition is impossible, stands the other extreme view, that monopoly power is impossible in manufacturing industries if unfair competition and special privileges be eliminated. There are, we are told, plenty of capital and plenty of business talent ready to enter any field where prices are high and profits promising. This is true in very considerable measure. The investigations of the Pujo committee, however, have made it clear that the flow of capital into industries is not altogether free from restraint. We may not credit fully the conclusions of that committee as to the power of the Money Trust. It is a fact, nevertheless, that a limited number of great financial interests, closely intertwined, and with a multitude of ramifications, have a considerable degree of control over credit throughout the country. A concern requiring large capital would find difficulty in placing securities or in borrowing money, if its purposes were inimical to combinations or corporations in which these great financial leaders were interested. At the same time, it must be admitted, the power of the Money Trust is by no means sufficient wholly to prevent new capital from entering into competition with the trusts.

Some take the position that the mere aggregation of great capital in the trust will implant such fear in the hearts of would-be competitors that they will keep out of the way. They urge that the great resources of the trust alone will enable it to survive losses of competition better than the smaller concern. With this view also I find myself unable to agree. The losses of a trust from competition reach a greater volume of business than those of the independent concern; proportionally they may be equally heavy. Only if the trust is more efficient than its competitors, or if it can use unfair methods of attacking them, is it able to drive them to the wall without itself suffering equally.

But does theory justify us in thinking that the trust will find it necessary to fight to the last ditch in order to rid itself of the competitors which are likely to spring up from time to time? Will not the same motives which led the group of competing concerns to combine at the outset appeal as well to the new competitors? It is by no means true, as some trust promoters would have us believe, that before the trusts were formed, destructive competition was causing intolerable losses. Usually the leading concerns were by no means in danger of the sheriff. They united because they saw the prospect of still greater gains than they were making. They felt it was more profitable to join in gouging the consumer than to try to get business away from one another. Will not the new concerns that rise up to plague the trusts find it convenient to do likewise after a reasonable period of competitive struggle?

We are not justified, on theoretical grounds, in anticipating any other history for the trust than that which has so often actually taken place in the past. The career of many, if not most, trusts has shown a wave movement. First, fairly complete elimination of competition and extortionate prices. Then an inroad of competition followed by moderate or low prices. Next the absorption of competitors, and high prices once more. What theoretic reason is there to believe that in the long run the average of prices under these fluctuations will be no higher than had there been no combination at all? What reason to suppose that during the periods of active competition the prices will go far below a profitable level? Can the trust induce its competitor to enter the sheltering arms of monopoly only after both have long been losing heavily?

Capital and talent may be ever ready to begin competition with the trusts. They are usually quite as ready to join with the trusts to keep up prices. Often the sole object of the new competitor is to break his way into the monopoly. It may not even be necessary for the combination to pay a very high price in order to buy him up. It may not be necessary to *buy* him up at all. He may simply agree with the trust to work in harmony, to follow its leadership.

But, it will be urged, the trusts will be able, by reason of their superior economy and efficiency, to secure profits, on the average, in excess of the normal competitive rate, and still charge prices at least as low as would be possible under a régime of general competition. Anticipating for a moment what will be discussed more fully in another lecture, we may note that superiority of the trusts in efficiency has been by many greatly overestimated. The trust may be more efficient than its smaller competitors as they actually exist today or than the separate plants that preceded the trust. That proves little. The things compared are not properly comparable. In most industries the trust possesses little superiority over large individual plants, or combinations of a less comprehensive character, such as would have arisen in the absence of the trust.

But even if the trust were the most efficient possible business unit, it does not follow that, in the absence of regulation of prices and profits by the government, the people could expect to share in the benefit of that efficiency. On the contrary, the efficiency itself might result to the injury of the public. It is by no means clear that the self-interest of trust managers would under such circumstances lead them to maintain prices uniformly low in order to keep competitors from entering the field. Might they not rather keep prices high as long as possible, relying on their ability to destroy competitors by underselling, whenever they arose? Might not the known ability of the trust to undersell without loss create such a fear that competition for long periods would not dare to raise its head? Superior efficiency of trusts may be an argument in favor of the policy of tolerating combinations subject to government regulation, but hardly in favor of a policy of *laissez faire.*

Experience and theory thus unite at least to warn us of the possible danger of trusts and pools. We cannot feel sure that the restriction of unfair competitive methods and the removal of special monopolistic privileges would rob them of power to mulct the consumer. Moreover, we have not yet been shown that it is possible to eradicate unfair competitive methods and special privileges. The government has been trying to put a stop to railroad discriminations for more than twenty years. It has reduced them greatly, but it has not wholly eliminated them. The task of preventing unfair methods of marketing goods would be even harder. It is easy to talk about prohibiting price discrimination, for example. Actually to prevent it would require elaborate administrative machinery. Price discrimination is practised more or less in almost every branch of industry and trade. Small concerns having no thought of monopoly often discriminate in prices. In some cases the practice is excusable if not desirable. Tho government would have grave difficulty in determining just where to draw the line. Indeed, to prove the fact of discrimination would often be virtually impossible, because of differences in the grade of goods sold, in the quantities sold to different purchasers, and in the costs of sale and delivery.

Difficult also would it be in many cases to deprive combinations of special monopoly privileges. For example, take patent rights. The patent possessed by a concern standing alone may give it only a limited degree of monopoly power. By combining with other concerns having patents for related machinery or processes the monopoly may become complete. We may prevent such combination by law. But if we permit it, how can we then deprive the combination of the added power which the pooling of patents gives? The only remedy for monopoly in that case would be regulation of the prices of the products. Again, a number of separate concerns having each part of a limited natural resource may unite so that they together control the entire resource or the greater part of it. This gives them an advantage over competitors that did not exist before. The combination might have been prevented, but if it is permitted the advantage thereby acquired with respect to the natural resource cannot be taken away save by the difficult method of government regulation of prices.

The restriction of unfair competitive methods and of special monopoly privileges would be a proper enough adjunct of the policy of prohibiting combinations, or of the policy of regulating their prices and profits. But standing alone it is not a sufficient safeguard against monopoly.

The solution of the trust problem, therefore, must be found either in prohibition or in regulation, not in *laissez faire*. Those who ask us to remove the ban of law from trusts and pools without substituting the controlling hand of government over prices are asking a departure from a policy that is as old as Anglo-Saxon civilization. They are asking us to leap into the dark. The results, tho conceivably not disastrous, might yet be extremely disastrous. The great majority of the American people have no desire to risk the experiment. I for one believe that they are right in refusing to do so.

CHAPTER II

THE POSSIBILITY OF PREVENTING COMBINATION

If the conclusion is reached that there is need for either regulation of combinations or prohibition of them, the question immediately arises whether the latter course is practicable. Can the government successfully break up existing combinations and prevent the formation of others ?

The limited experience of this country thus far in "trust busting" is often cited as proving the impossibility of destroying the trusts. In some cases the so-called dissolutions have in fact failed to bring about real competition. Yet in some other instances a considerable measure of competition has apparently been restored. As regards the great majority of the cases no information concerning the results is available. So little time has elapsed since the anti-trust laws began to be enforced with some vigor that a pessimistic judgment as to the ultimate outcome is premature. Moreover, the methods of dealing with the combinations thus far have been relatively gentle and the results do not justify a conclusion as to what might be accomplished by a really rigorous policy of repression.

The opinions of most people concerning the results accomplished under the Sherman anti-trust act are based on a few conspicuous cases. They do not even know that there have been scores of prosecutions and suits in equity under that act, the great majority of which have been decided in favor of the government. While the earliest decisions of the Supreme Court tended greatly to narrow the scope of the Sherman law, later decisions have turned increasingly in the other direction. The court has not only upheld the constitutionality of the act in every respect, but it has held its broad terminology applicable to almost — but not quite — every specific form of combination or of contract in restraint of trade, and to almost every monopolistic practice of which complaint is made. Supposed rights of property and of contract have in considerable measure been brushed aside by the court when urged as a defense for monopoly. The Sherman Act needs comparatively little modification with respect to its scope and its definitions. The state courts also have shown vigor in enforcing the various state anti-trust laws.

Yet repression has not thus far taken drastic form. It is one thing for the courts to adopt a broad policy in holding a combination, contract or practice unlawful. It is quite another to use vigorous measures to punish it or prevent its recurrence. Thus far there has been scarcely a single instance of imprisonment for violation of either state or federal anti-trust laws. Juries have not shown a disposition to convict where imprisonment was the necessary penalty, or where they believed that the judges would probably impose that penalty. Where judges have had a choice between fining and imprisoning offenders, they have uniformly inflicted the fine. In fact, many of the fines have been unreasonably light, in some cases far less than the profits which the combination had gained through violation of the law.

It would have been harsh to imprison men in the first campaign against the trusts under the Sherman law.

The law had long been allowed to remain a dead letter. Business men generally did not look upon monopolistic combinations or practices as immoral. Hence administrative officers, judges and juries were justified in leniency. It does not follow that leniency is desirable for the future, or that the people will be disposed to tolerate it. Now that the public has shown that it means business in attacking combinations and monopolies, and that the meaning of the laws is clearly established and generally known, men who form combinations, make contracts in restraint of trade, or pursue monopolistic practices, know that they do so at their peril, and severe punishments will be perfectly proper. If necessary, the anti-trust laws could be so amended as to make imprisonment the only penalty in criminal cases, or to increase greatly the minimum and maximum fines. A vigorous enforcement of anti-trust laws, especially by imposing prison sentences, would virtually stop the more formal combinations and contracts in restraint of trade as well as the more obvious methods of unfair competition. The average business man fears the jail mightily. Very few are deliberate law-breakers. Tho some secret combinations in plain violation of the laws might be attempted even in the face of severe punishment if discovered, they would probably be very few. The question whether informal understandings could be prevented and whether genuine and active competition could be brought about is, however, different and will be considered later.

A large proportion of the proceedings under the Sherman act have not been criminal indictments, but bills in equity seeking injunctions. In a few cases the same combination has been pursued both criminally and in equity. The injunction is under certain conditions a very necessary device for enforcing the statute. It is difficult to see how a closely knit trust like the Standard Oil Company could be satisfactorily broken up without an order of the court as to the method of doing so. Merely to impose penalties upon a trust or its managers, and to leave them to devise means of dissolving it, would often open the door for endless litigation among the members and stockholders of the combination. A pool, a contract in restraint of trade, a monopolistic practice can be discontinued forthwith. In attacking these, a prosecuting officer has his choice between criminal and equity proceedings. An injunction against them does little to add to the effectiveness of the penal provisions of the law itself. But the dissolution of a trust or corporate combination requires positive and not merely negative action. It takes time and skill. It calls for decrees in equity.

Most of the cases under the Sherman act have been not against trusts proper, but against pools, contracts in restraint of trade, and monopolistic practices. There is reason to believe that much has been accomplished in cases of this type, tho positive evidence is for the most part lacking. Very seldom have the courts been asked to punish the same offenders a second time, or to find them guilty of contempt in violating injunctions. It is perfectly easy for the separate concerns which agreed together in a pool and which theretofore were competitors to resume competition. In the past many a pool has dissolved itself, or fallen asunder without legal action. I have no doubt whatever that most of the pools, contracts in restraint of trade and monopolistic practices against which the law has been invoked have actually been discontinued in form, and a good many of them in substance.

In the more familiar cases against the Northern Securities, Standard Oil and American Tobacco combinations, the court had to deal with holding companies. The oil and tobacco trusts in particular were not mere assemblages of separate concerns. Each was a working, organic unity. The Standard Oil combination had been in existence for forty years. Most of the constituent corporations whose stocks were controlled by the Standard Oil Company of New Jersey had never been independent; they were children of the parent concern by birth and not by adoption. The separate corporations were maintained merely for legal convenience. Very few of the men who managed them had ever had experience with competition against one another. The tobacco trust was but little less firmly knit together.

To establish competition among the parts of the oil and tobacco trusts was thus of necessity a difficult task by any method. The method actually pursued by the courts in these cases was wholly inadequate to the situation. Indeed, that method was not adequate even for the much easier task of breaking up the combination of railroads formed under the Northern Securities Company, a combination in which each railroad was a distinct entity and not an essential member of a unified whole.

In each of these three cases the decree of the court permitted the holding corporation to divide the shares of the various constituent companies *pro rata* among the stockholders of the holding company. A person who held one-tenth of the stock of the Standard Oil Company of New Jersey, for example, became thereafter the holder of one-tenth of the stock of each of the former subsidiary companies. To be sure, the decree prohibited the use of liquidating certificates or other evidences of joint ownership in two or more of the subsidiaries, as well as other formal devices for securing unity of control. The several companies, their officers, and directors were enjoined from agreeing together as to the conduct of business in such a way as to restrain trade. There was no prohibition, however, against the election of the same persons as directors or officers of two or more of the companies.

It is difficult to see why it should be anticipated that changes in the ownership of the stock thus distributed would take place, within any reasonable length of time, such as would destroy the substantial community of interest. John D. Rockefeller had owned about one-fourth of the stock of the Standard Oil Company of New Jersey. A very small number of men had controlled a majority of the stock. These same men now control a majority of the stocks of the segregated companies. What possible motive have they for selling stocks in one of the companies rather than in another? Rather is it to be expected that they, and their heirs after them, will in general continue to hold all of these stocks, or, if they do dispose of any, will dispose of equal proportions in each of the companies. Changes are perhaps more likely to take place in the ownership of the smaller blocks of shares; but these have no influence in the control of corporations. So long as there is a community of ownership in the shares, formal agreement among the several corporations of the Standard Oil group regarding prices, output or other matters is by no means necessary to insure substantial harmony in operation. No man naturally competes against himself.

The situation with respect to the former constituent companies of the Northern Securities Company and the American Tobacco Company is the same as with respect to the Standard companies.

This method of dissolving trusts, — by leaving the ownership of all the constituent parts to the same persons that owned the former controlling corporation, — can hardly be characterized by any other word than farcical. It rests on the false assumption that a corporation has motives and ideas different from those of the persons who own it. The courts have repeatedly asserted that, in judging of the existence or the legality of a combination in restraint of trade, they must and will look beneath mere forms, and will consider the essence, the purpose of the men who conspire beneath the cloak of the corporation. In making the decrees of dissolution in these leading trust cases, however, the courts have dealt with form rather than with substance.

There would be no insuperable difficulty in adopting a more effective method of dissolving such closely-knit trusts. The stockholders of the controlling corporation could be required to apportion the securities or properties held by it among themselves in such a way that no one should have an interest in more than a single part. Such a method of dissolution might not immediately restore competition, but it would at least render competition possible and ultimately probable. Of course, the procedure suggested would not be altogether easy. There might be bickerings among the stockholders as to the relative values of the several constituent parts, particularly in view of the fact that such values after the dissolution of the combination might bear a different relation to one another from those obtaining under the combination. If the court or the administrative authorities had to undertake the task of valuing the constituent properties for the purpose of such dissolution, much expert investigation would be required. But the thing is quite possible. It involves little more difficulty or more likelihood of injustice than is involved in the valuation of stocks and properties of constituent concerns at the time they enter a combination. The managers of the trust itself could be required to take the initiative in working out such a scheme of dissolution.

I do not propose to discuss the constitutionality of such a procedure. However, the increasing liberality of the courts in putting the public interest above the rights of property seems to hold a promise that they might uphold a provision of law requiring such a method of dissolution of monopolistic holding companies and prohibiting community of stock ownership where it tends to monopoly. If some injury resulted to investors it would be proper to remind them that when they entered into an unlawful combination, or bought its securities, they knowingly incurred the risk of loss through government intervention. Surely it would be strange if the law should avail to fine or imprison those who form a trust and yet be powerless to effect a real dissolution of such a combination.

In this connection it is worthy of note that the decree of the Court in the recent Union Pacific case did not authorize the distribution of the shares of the Southern Pacific Company held by the Union Pacific among the stockholders of the latter. The decree declared that such stock should be disposed of only with the approval of the Court. As a matter of fact, a large block of the Southern Pacific stock was turned over to the Pennsylvania Railroad.

As may be inferred from the preceding discussion, I do not believe any important measure of competition exists today among the companies which formerly were controlled by the Northern Securities, oil, and tobacco combinations. It is not in human nature that it should exist under the conditions. Moreover, there is no outward evidence that competition has been restored as a result of the decrees in these three cases. It is true that a very active campaign of advertising has recently been conducted by the companies into which the tobacco trust was divided, but this does not necessarily mean competition among them. Even in the days of its strongest hold on the trade, the American Tobacco Company was a great advertiser, both for the purpose of maintaining the popularity of its brands as against outside competitors and for the purpose of stimulating consumption.

We must conclude, therefore, that, until we have tried more vigorous measures than have been thus far employed, despair as to the possibility of restoring competition among the constituents of a trust is unwarranted.

Difficult as it may be to break up trusts already formed and firmly knit together, there seems no serious difficulty in preventing by law the formation of new trusts. Indeed, it is noteworthy that since the government began somewhat actively to bring proceedings under the Sherman anti-trust act, almost no trusts have been organized. If a proper control over the organization of corporations and over their acquisition of property and securities were exercised by the states and by the federal government, the attempt to organize new trusts could be nipped in the bud. Herein lies one of the strongest justifications for the creation of the new federal trade commission.

It would appear from the preceding discussion that there is no serious difficulty in destroying and preventing by law the more formal pools and contracts in restraint of trade, or in preventing the formation of new trusts; nor even any insuperable difficulty in effectively breaking up trusts already organized. There remains the question whether, in the absence of formal combinations and contracts in restraint of trade, those of an informal character, which the law cannot reach, will persist and will possess the power seriously to injure the public. It is, of course, impossible to compel people to compete, in the sense of attempting, by the lowering of prices or otherwise, to get all the trade they can. The law cannot punish concerns each of which, without any written or oral agreement, takes merely the business which comes to it at the prices which it considers fair.

Those who believe it impossible to maintain competition in modern industry urge that the losses from unregulated competition are so severe that business men and investors will do everything possible to escape them. They point to the experience of the railroads. Railroad rate wars often reduced the competing lines to poverty or bankruptcy, and all but forced them into pools. The fierceness of railroad competition is due primarily to the fact that the transportation business is, at least up to a certain point in density of traffic, one of increasing returns. This tempts each company to increase its business at almost any cost. Moreover, it is impossible for the railroad to withdraw its investment, however unprofitable it may become. It is urged that manufacturing industries in which large fixed capital is required present substantially similar conditions in both respects. To the manufacturing establishment also, if it has large investment in plant, the fullest possible operation means the lowest interest cost per unit of output. In industries not requiring much fixed capital, it is possible for the competitor to withdraw if the business become unprofitable, thus setting a limit to the disastrous effects of competition. In industries with large fixed capital, we are told, it is impossible for any one to withdraw. Consequently, the concern which is losing most from competition will continue to cut prices, in the hope of gaining enough business to pay expenses and prevent absolute loss of the investment. Thus, it is contended, the business of all competitors often becomes unprofitable, and the temptation to combine, for restoring and maintaining prices, becomes well-nigh irresistible.

If the conditions were as serious as thus depicted, we should feel disposed not merely to give up the struggle to maintain competition in our leading industries, but even to encourage combination. Persistent loss from excessive competition is intolerable. Among well-informed and unbiased observers, there has, therefore, developed a strong feeling in favor of permitting pooling and community of interest among railroads.

But is it true that competition in manufacturing industries tends ordinarily to such extreme lengths? Are the conditions in any appreciable number of industries closely similar to those in railroad transportation? This seems to me not proved.

In the first place, in most industries, the relative importance of fixed capital is much lower than with the railroads and other public service industries. The capital investment of the railroads of the United States is between four and five times as great as their gross annual revenue. The capital investment of the gas companies and of the electric light companies bears about the same ratio to their gross earnings. On the other hand, in manufacturing industries taken as a whole, the census returns show a capital investment less than the annual value of product.[1] Even in the steel industry, which is one of exceptionally large fixed capital, the reported value of capital only slightly exceeds the annual value of output. The statistics on which these statements are based are not altogether reliable, but they do show approximately the true relations. Again, the principle of increasing returns in the case of railroads extends in large measure even to operating costs; this is seldom true of manufacturing concerns. For these reasons to reduce the output of a manufacturing plant when prices are unfavorable does not in most cases increase unit costs, including capital charges, to any such extent as in transportation. Finally, in railroad competition there are usually only a few lines involved. Each of them may readily have sufficient capacity to handle the whole competitive business. In most manufacturing industries, on the

[1] This statement with regard to manufacturing industries is based upon the census of 1909, which gives the value of capital as $18,428,000,000 and the value of products as $20,672,000,000. The latter item involves much duplication, due to the use of the products of one plant as material for another; but it is proper to compare this gross value with that of the capital. For if a manufacturing concern shuts down in order to avoid loss, it eliminates its entire cost of materials, whether strictly raw materials or the partly finished product of other manufacturing concerns.

other hand, plants are numerous. The individual plant has but a comparatively small fraction of the total capacity. Under such conditions no one plant can by price cutting expect to increase its share of the business in any such proportion as the railroad can.

For these reasons, competition of a really destructive kind is much less likely to arise in manufacturing industries than in railroad transportation. It follows that the motive for combination is less powerful in the former than in the latter. There are many manufacturing industries today in which we find neither destructive competition nor combinations in restraint of competition.

In any case, even tho the desire to suppress competition be strong among business men in manufacturing industries, it is very difficult effectively to suppress it when combination is under the ban of the law. Informal agreements and tacit understandings are far less effective in stopping competition than the more formal and definite combinations which it is proposed to prohibit. It is not easy for a group of separate concerns to act in harmony, to refrain from competition. This is particularly the case when prices are at a high level. If each concern could be sure that its competitor was maintaining prices and not seeking to get a larger proportion of the business, tacit combination might go on peacefully. But the temptation to shade prices and get business away from others is always strong. The mere unfounded suspicion that competitors are pursuing this policy often leads the business man to seek to protect his trade by lowering prices, or by other competitive measures. If once the bars are let down anywhere, the whole trade is likely to rush into the field of active competition.

The history of combinations in the past is full of efforts to make them more binding, more cohesive, to prevent more effectively the internal competition that would ever break forth. Agreements as to prices were found ineffective without systematic measures for dividing output or profits. Agreements for such pooling of business or profits broke down unless there was efficient machinery for enforcing them, backed by heavy penalties. Despite even such vigorous methods, many of the pools were not strong enough to prevent competition among their own members. It was largely for this reason that the original trust form of organization, and later the corporate combination, became popular. The difficulties which the railroads in the earlier days encountered in their efforts to suppress competition among themselves are well known; and this despite the fact that their managers knew the peculiar risk of heavy losses from rate wars. The conditions which made competition so disastrous, which offered such an incentive to combination, themselves rendered the prevention of competition peculiarly difficult. No doubt, a large majority of business men would prefer to combine with one another in order to exact high prices from the public. It has already been suggested that if combination were freely permitted, competition would very likely be eliminated in large degree. But combination under the ban of the law is a very different thing from combination with its sanction.

Those who hold that it is impossible to maintain competition as a general basis of business are called on to explain the fact that competition does exist today in a large proportion of the field of production and trade. Many as are the more formal combinations, perhaps even more numerous the informal understandings among business concerns, there are wide fields in which real competition exists. Can any one deny, for example, that the mining of bituminous coal, or the manufacture of cotton goods, of boots and shoes, of automobiles, is conducted under essentially competitive conditions ? Is not the same true of a large part of the wholesale and retail merchandizing ? The advantages of combination to its members are so well known that we should expect to find competition practically eliminated everywhere, were it not for the real difficulties of eliminating it.

There is, therefore, no occasion for despair as to the suppression of trusts and pools. Monopoly is not inevitable. Competition in manufacturing and mercantile business is not so destructive as to force combination. The failure of some of the so-called trust dissolutions to restore competition is no proof that more rational and more vigorous methods of enforcing the law would also fail to do so. Competition has been restored in some cases where monopoly once reigned. In many important industries competition has never succumbed.

Hence we can consider on their merits the relative advantages of trust prohibition and trust regulation. Our choice is not foreclosed by the impracticability of the former. Is a trust régime superior from the standpoint of efficiency to a régime of competition ? Is it possible effectively to regulate the prices and profits of trusts ? What would be the ultimate consequences of a policy of regulation ? These questions remain to be discussed.

CHAPTER III

DIFFICULTIES OF REGULATING COMBINATIONS

In the preceding lectures we have undertaken to show that it is necessary either to prohibit and destroy the trusts and pools or to regulate their prices and profits. Merely to prohibit unfair competitive methods and to deprive combinations of special privileges would not, in all probability, remove their power to extort monopoly prices. We further sought to show that it is possible to prevent the formation of combinations having effective monopoly power, and possible also in large measure to break up such combinations as already exist. The American people, therefore, are in a position to choose between the policy of regulating permitted trusts and pools, and the policy of prohibiting and destroying them. In making this choice they must first consider what would be the difficulties and what the probable results of a policy of regulation. They must then consider whether the advantages of combinations from the standpoint of efficiency and economy are great enough to justify permitting them to exist despite the difficulties of regulating them.

Few of those who have advocated the policy of permitting combinations to exist subject to regulation by the government seem to have given much thought to the magnitude of such a task, its difficulties, or its ultimate outcome. They have had in mind the comparatively few closely knit trusts of the present time, or possibly only a part of those trusts. They have had in mind particularly the so-called "good" trusts with their alleged superior efficiency and their more or less reasonable policy toward the public.

In the first place, it would be difficult to limit the number of trusts under such a policy. It is, of course, conceivable that the government should undertake to suppress combinations in general, while permitting a few particular trusts to exist. A limited number of trusts might be tolerated, not because of the good motives or exceptional ability of their managers, but because of special economic characteristics of the industries concerned which tended to make combination particularly economical or to make the maintenance of competition peculiarly difficult. Such a plan would not necessarily lead to unreasonable discrimination between individuals and classes, tho to determine what were the extraordinary conditions justifying the existence of a trust would be extremely hard. If, however, the people once concede the right of a monopolistic combination to exist, independently of extraordinary conditions, a sense of justice should apparently compel them to permit combinations *ad libitum.* What is sauce for the goose is sauce for the gander. Under no theory of justice could all the trusts heretofore organized be permitted to continue without granting permission to organize trusts in every other field. Moreover, if the government permitted trusts freely to organize, it would have to permit pools also, at least until it was demonstrated that the trusts had material economies and other advantages and that the pools had no such advantages.

In the second place, it would seem that if combinations having power to restrain trade are to be permitted at all, they must be permitted to become as comprehensive as they desire. Why should a combination not be allowed to take over 100 per cent of the business in its field quite as readily as 90 or 80 or 70 per cent? Very few persons desire to prohibit combinations which control only a small proportion of a given industry and which possess no possible monopoly power; but if we permit that limit to be overstepped at all, there is no limit.

One can only speculate how numerous and how comprehensive the trusts and pools would become if the policy were adopted of permitting them freely but subjecting them to regulation. Presumably the disinclination to submit themselves to government regulation would prevent business men from forming combinations as universally as they would if combinations were permitted without regulation. It is quite possible that the field of combination would become immensely great. In all probability it would become far greater than at present. Beyond question, moreover, every combination, unless prevented by the government, would take in just as large a proportion of the trade as could be persuaded to enter it. In many cases this would mean the entire trade.

If combinations were freely permitted and no limit placed upon their magnitude, neither actual nor potential competition would be an adequate check upon prices and charges for service. This was, I think, sufficiently demonstrated in the first lecture. Government regulation would unquestionably be necessary.

Some have suggested that regulation would be comparatively simple. Good trusts would be left alone and only bad trusts interfered with, and the fear of government intervention would make most of the trusts good. The government, some seem to think, could let the trust go its own way until it was proved to have become extortionate or to have used unfair competitive methods, and could then step in and punish its officers, or suspend its right to do business for a season, or even dissolve it altogether. Such a course is fundamentally inconsistent with the principle of permitting combinations at all. How is the trust manager to know in advance what prices or what practices will be adjudged so unreasonable as to call for criminal prosecution? What advantage would there be in breaking up a trust the first time it went too far, if another trust could be formed in its place the next day? It would be intolerable to the users of the products or the services of a trust to stop its business, even temporarily, as a punishment for unreasonable prices or unfair methods of competition. A good trust may become a bad trust overnight. Shall it be a lawful organization today and an outlawed wreck tomorrow? Regulation of combinations implies continuity of the combinations.

Even if the government adopted the policy of punishing trust managers or breaking up combinations, as a penalty for extortionate prices and unfair practices, it would require almost as thoro and continuous investigation and quite as difficult judgment on the part of the government to determine when to inflict such penalties as to determine the proper prices and practices for the future. It would be most unjust to take drastic action against a trust or its managers without possession of most detailed knowledge of all the conditions.

In its very essence, however, regulation implies, not

punishment of past action, but prescription of future action. This means simply that the government, if it undertakes to regulate the trusts and combinations, will ultimately have to fix their prices or limit their profits, or both. After all, the one thing in which the general public is interested is the reasonableness of prices and charges. The prevention of combinations in restraint of trade and of unfair competitive methods are not ends in themselves. There is no way to insure reasonable prices under monopoly except to restrict them, — to fix them outright, or to limit the profits in such a way as to remove the incentive to unreasonable prices.

If the government enters upon the policy of fixing prices and profits strictly, ought it not to go a step further and guarantee to the combinations a permanent monopoly, protecting them against competition? It has long been urged by the owners of railroads and other public service industries that justice to investors demands protection against competition as a concomitant of regulation of rates and charges. The public has been gradually coming to accept this view. If for a series of years the investor in trust securities has had his profits held down to a low percentage by government regulation, it is hardly fair for the government to permit those profits to be still further lowered, perhaps wholly destroyed, by the advent of a competitor.

Whatever might be the outcome of government regulation in this respect, there can be no doubt of the immense difficulty of just and efficient regulation of the prices or the profits of industrial combinations. As already shown, the field to be covered by regulation would probably be exceedingly wide and diverse. The federal government and the states would have to maintain elaborate and powerful machinery to control the combinations. The task of regulation could not possibly be left to the courts, lacking as they are in the necessary machinery for investigation and occupied as they are with many other duties.

Consider for a moment the nature of the task which would confront such an administrative body. In the first place, it would have to possess at all times detailed information regarding all the concerns under its jurisdiction. It could not rest content with making special investigations from time to time on its own initiative or on complaint. Railroad rates and the charges of public service corporations are ordinarily comparatively stable, and properly so; but the prices of many other commodities, if not of most, are necessarily variable. The costs of materials may change greatly and rapidly. The conditions of demand are changeable. Grave injury might be done to the public during the time required for securing information on which to base action if such information were not continuously in the possession of the regulating authority. Even annual reports would not usually be adequate; quarterly or monthly data would be required.

In the second place, the amount of detail involved would be enormous. A proper fixing of prices would require complete knowledge of the costs of production and of the amount of investment. In order to make sure of obtaining accurate information, the government would have to prescribe the methods of accounting. It would be impossible to prescribe uniform methods, as is done by the Interstate Commerce Commission in the case of the railroads. The bewildering variety of conditions in the different industries would have to be provided for. On the basis of accounting methods thus prescribed, detailed reports would have to be made to the government and these would have to be scrutinized and studied with utmost care. The federal government particularly would have to employ a vast corps of expert accountants, statisticians, and specialists familiar with the peculiar conditions in the different industries.

The difficulties of cost accounting are so great that many even of the largest business concerns have found it impossible to ascertain the costs of their products on scientific principles, or at any rate have considered it not worth while to incur the necessary expenses for that purpose. The business concern can get along without accurate knowledge of its own costs. Its prime interest is in demand and in profits. The government, however, in fixing prices, must know all about costs — both operating costs and capital charges. They are the very things which primarily determine the reasonableness of prices. The limiting of profits would require somewhat less detailed information than the limiting of prices, but would still require a vast mass of data.

In the third place, the determination of costs and of investment for the purpose of fixing prices or profits would involve immensely difficult problems of judgment. The judgment of the regulating body would be constantly challenged by the combinations and the probable result would be endless litigation. The proper allowance for depreciation and obsolescence, the proper apportionment of overhead charges among different products and services, the proper methods of valuing the different elements of investment, — these and similar matters would have to be passed upon by the regulating authority. Such problems are difficult enough as they confront the Interstate Commerce Commission, which has to deal with one kind of business only. They would be far more difficult for a body dealing with multifarious combinations in widely differing industries.

Even if the regulating authority should succeed in working out a satisfactory determination of costs of production and value of investment, it would still be beset with troubles in fixing prices or limiting profits. Demand for goods is variable even in non-competitive industries. Even if the combinations should be protected against competition from domestic concerns, foreign concerns would have to be reckoned with. Unchanging prices or prices bearing an unchanging relation to costs would not be practicable in mining, manufacturing and mercantile business. A combination might at times be justified in reducing prices and consequently profits below a normal level in order to stimulate demand and keep its force employed, or in order to meet foreign competition. The government would have then to determine to what limit prices or profits could subsequently be advanced in order to offset these reductions. In other words, the government would be dealing with a constantly changing problem of demand, just as the manager of any private business does.

Particularly difficult would be the fixing of proper prices for products produced at joint cost. Take petroleum, for example. A wide variety of commodities are derived from the one raw material, crude oil. Some of these are in so little demand that they must be sold for less than the price of crude oil itself. Others are in great demand and can be sold for high prices. It is impossible to use cost as a basis for determining prices of the specific products. The relative demand for the several products varies from day to day. For a regulating body to determine the proper relationship of the prices of these joint products is virtually impossible. This and several other important industries would have to be regulated, if at all, by limiting profits rather than prices.

It is sometimes suggested that the same problem of joint costs confronts the Interstate Commerce Commission with respect to the relative freight rates on different commodities. It should be noted, however, that after making due allowance for actual and measurable differences in the cost of transporting different commodities, the Commission could, without actually destroying railroad business, fix precisely the same rate per unit for every class of commodities. Such a policy is by no means unthinkable and might be better than the often extraordinary differences which now exist. For petroleum products on the other hand, — and the same is true of a good many other products similarly produced under joint cost, — flat prices would be absolutely impossible. Furthermore, it cannot be said that the Interstate Commerce Commission has satisfactorily solved the problem of fixing relative rates on different commodities. It has in fact left that problem almost untouched, and if it ever does enter seriously upon it, the Commission may find difficulties practically insuperable.

One could continue almost indefinitely setting forth the complexities and difficulties of government regulation of the prices and profits of combinations. Most people feel that for the government actually to fix definite prices for a multitude of industries, or even to limit their profits specifically, would be impracticable. Many advocates of government regulation hope somehow to get along in a more rough and ready manner. They vaguely contemplate a vague form of regulation. They expect the government to exercise a general restraining influence, to intervene occasionally and to render its judgments in a more or less hit and miss fashion. They hope that with the hand of the government resting upon them, as it were, in a general sort of way, and with potential competition also exercising some restraining influence, the combinations for the most part will behave themselves decently. They count upon the alleged superior efficiency of the trusts in production and marketing to counterbalance the ineffectiveness and incompleteness of regulation.

Doubtless we could get along after a fashion with such a superficial form of regulation as this. It would be difficult, however, to prove that the public would be any better off under such a régime of half-regulated monopoly than under a régime of competition enforced as well as possible by laws against combinations and monopolies. Remove once the fear of penalties or of dissolution, and the combinations would always be crowding the limit of public tolerance. On the average, and in the long run, their prices and charges might not be greatly above a fair level, but they would almost certainly be somewhat above that level. Combination must be proved decidedly more efficient than competition before the people would be justified in trusting trusts under any but most rigid government control.

The work of the Interstate Commerce Commission in regulating railroads is often held up as demonstrating the practicability of successful government regulation of trusts. It has already been shown, however, that the regulation of trusts would be a much more complex task than the regulation of railroads. Moreover, with all due respect to the great intelligence and fairness with which the Interstate Commerce Commission has discharged its duties, we may yet question whether the ability of the Commission to regulate the railroads satisfactorily has been put to a final test. The Commission has thus far been concerned chiefly with the relationship of rates between different places. It has corrected many abuses in this respect, tho many still remain. As already stated, it has done very little to change the relation between the rates on different commodities, a relation which is often unreasonable. The commission has never had to face the problem of reducing the general level of rates for all railroads or for any particular railroad. The enormous increase in the volume of traffic during recent years would have enabled the railroads to obtain altogether unreasonable profits under existing rates, had it not been for the coincidence of a great advance in the prices of commodities and in the costs of railroad operation. Had this not happened, the Commission would have been called upon to reduce rates in a wholesale manner and it would have found that task immensely complicated, besides encountering tremendous opposition from the railroads and the many who sympathize with them. The task recently and still before the Commission, of determining whether, or by how much, railroads shall be permitted to advance rates is a far easier task than that of compelling a general lowering of rates.

Government regulation of prices and profits of private concerns always involves a large element of waste, of duplication of energy and cost. It means that two sets of persons are concerning themselves with the same work. The managers and employees of the corporations must study cost accounts and conditions of demand in determining price policy. The officers and employees of the government must follow and do it all over again. Moreover, the fact that these two sets of persons have different motives in approaching their work means friction and litigation, and these spell further expense. To superimpose a vast governmental machinery upon the vast machinery of private business is an extravagance which should be avoided if it is possible to do so.

The policy of government regulation of industry may readily become a stepping stone to government ownership and socialism. The chances are strong that the government of the United States will take over the telegraphs and telephones in the near future and the railroads within less than half a century. The demand for government ownership of these as well as of municipal public utilities may come from various sources. If regulation by the government proves ineffective in securing reasonable rates and charges, the general public will demand government ownership. If regulation proves so effective as to leave only moderate returns to the stockholders of the corporations, the stockholders are likely to urge government purchase, which would at least assure them of a more certain income. In either case the excessive cost of government regulation will be urged as a reason for government ownership. In the same way, if the government undertakes detailed regulation of combinations in manufacturing, mining and trade, there is bound to be a strong movement for government ownership in these fields also.

Government ownership of this or that industry is not necessarily a bad thing. Even government ownership of a large proportion of the industries of the country, nay, even complete socialism, need not necessarily affright us. To discuss the merits of government ownership would take us too far afield. It is sufficient merely to point out that the people ought not to enter on the path of permitting and regulating combinations without considering the advantages and disadvantages of this, the possible ultimate outcome, as well as those of the immediate policy itself. If it could be proved that combination is materially more economical than competition, we should doubtless be wise to say farewell to competition. Presumably in that case we ought to test thoroly the practicability of government regulation of private monopoly before proceeding further. The people would naturally first try the plan of government ownership, if at all, in limited fields, and compare the results with those under regulated monopoly before undertaking general government ownership. It is by no means improbable that the ultimate outcome would be socialism. The future is very likely to see either a régime of general competition, — with, of course, some special exceptions, — or a régime of universal communism. Clearly then we should be very sure of our ground before we take the first step toward possible communism. We should convince ourselves beyond all doubt that competition is impossible; or that, if possible, it is less efficient than monopoly, — not merely at certain times and in certain places, but generally and permanently, — before we tolerate widespread combination in the field of business.

We have not referred here to the effects of regulation upon the trusts themselves. We have considered only the difficulties which the government would encounter in an attempt to regulate trusts. It is quite possible that regulation would largely destroy that very efficiency which is held up as the reason for permitting them to exist. The discussion of this topic, however, belongs more properly with the next lecture, in which the alleged superior efficiency of trusts will be considered in detail.

CHAPTER IV

THE ALLEGED ADVANTAGES OF COMBINATION

In the preceding lecture we have tried to show that regulation of the prices and profits of trusts and pools would involve much difficulty. Nevertheless, if it could be shown that combinations controlling a large proportion of their respective industries were necessary to secure the highest economy and efficiency, and possessed other economic advantages, the proper course would be to permit such combinations, while subjecting them to regulation.

Claims of this sort are put forth with much vigor in behalf of the trusts. We are told by many that the trust is a natural evolution, that it is the last word in industrial progress, that to destroy it would be to turn the hands of the clock backward. Let us restrict monopolistic greed, they say; let us, if necessary, destroy the bad trusts; but let us not lose the advantages of good and efficient trusts. Some go further and descant on the evils, nay, the immorality, of competition, the superiority of peace over the sword in industry as in international politics. War is hell; competition is war, say they.

The claim that the trust possesses superior efficiency deserves thoro and fair consideration. The assertion that the desire for greater efficiency was the primary motive in the organization of the trusts, however, is not in accordance with the facts. The trust was far from being a natural sequence in the progress of methods of production. In a sense, everything that happens in economic history is a natural evolution. It is due to the working of laws. But in the sense in which trust defenders use the phrase, the trust movement in the United States was anything but a natural evolution. It was essentially artificial. The basic motive for the organization of most trusts was to suppress competition, to maintain or advance prices. Hostile criticism from without was met by the proclamation of other motives and the prophecy of other results. Within the camp, talk was all of the advantages of checking competition. That was the appeal to the owners of the concerns which were invited to enter the fold. That was the appeal to the investors in securities. Indeed, many of the leaders in the trust movement admitted frankly to the public, — before the Industrial Commission of 1899, for example, — that desire to check so-called destructive competition was their original incentive.

A second important factor in the organization of trusts, particularly during the most active period of trust formation from 1898 to 1901, was the desire for profits of promotion and of speculation. The promoter with his glib tongue and glowing prospectus was very much in evidence. There was a craze for combination among business men and investors. Over-capitalization was a practically universal feature of the corporate combinations of this period. Over-capitalization was designed in part to conceal from the public the profits of operation. Even more, its purpose was to help promoters unload properties upon the investing public at high valuations.

The fact that the trust movement was largely based on illegitimate motives and fostered by artificial methods does not demonstrate that trusts are disadvantageous to the general public, but it should at least dim the halo of sanctity with which some seek to surround them. It places them on the defensive.

The main argument in favor of the trusts, their supposed superior efficiency and economy, can scarcely be advanced in behalf of the pools. To affect costs materially, the combination must control fully all the operations of its constituent concerns. This the pool does not attempt to do. In fact, very few of the advocates of trusts attempt to defend pools. Yet should the policy of permitting combinations to exist be adopted, it would be found difficult, constitutionally and practically, to draw a rigid line between permitted trusts and prohibited pools.

Most of the discussions of trust efficiency, whether based on statistics and other facts of experience or on general reasoning, do not go to the true issue and therefore do not prove anything. It has been assumed that to show that a great combination of plants is more efficient than a single plant is to show the desirability of trusts. Far from it. The advocate of trusts must prove further the superiority of the trust, — that is, the combination sufficiently comprehensive to possess or at least to threaten monopolistic power, — over the smaller combination possessing no possible monopolistic power. He must show either that combinations increase in efficiency merely with increase in magnitude, or that the elimination of competition itself is necessary to the highest efficiency. Very few propose to prohibit combinations altogether; usually it is only monopolistic or potentially monopolistic combinations that are attacked.

The investigations of trusts hitherto conducted have been quite inadequate to prove whether or not they are the most efficient organization for conducting business. It is sometimes argued, therefore, that the people should defer judgment regarding the trusts pending further investigation of their efficiency. Some go so far as to suggest that the government undertake to determine for each industry the exact point at which the size of combinations reaches the limit of economy in production and marketing. It is doubtful whether further investigations along these lines would be especially instructive. Serious difficulties stand in the way of reaching definite conclusions from them.

Even an effort to compare the efficiency of a trust régime with that of a régime of strictly separate plants and entire absence of combination holds little prospect of success. An investigation on this point might be undertaken in either of three ways. It might compare conditions in a given industry before and after the formation of the trust. It might compare the business of the trust with that of independent concerns in the same industry at the same time. It might compare trusts with independent concerns in other industries. Either of these methods of investigation encounters great obstacles from lack of cost data. So difficult is it to calculate costs accurately that many concerns, particularly those operating only a single plant, have not yet undertaken thoro-going cost accounting. Very few, indeed, of the plants which entered into the trusts had satisfactory cost accounts before that time and such accounts as did exist are in most cases no longer accessible.

But suppose by following the first of the methods of inquiry above mentioned it should be shown that, after taking into account changes in the prices of materials and in wages, a trust today was doing business more cheaply than its predecessor concerns ten or fifteen or twenty years ago. Would that prove the increase in efficiency to be due to combination? Efficiency has advanced also in industries where no combinations have been organized. This is the era of the cost accountant and the efficiency engineer. During recent years business men inside and outside of combinations have been applying themselves to bettering methods more assiduously than ever before. Increased size of plants, larger and better machinery, better methods of organization are characteristic of practically every industry. The census statistics as to the average number of employees and of horse power per establishment seem to indicate that, while increase in average size of plants is perhaps more conspicuous in industries where the trusts are prominent, there is no marked difference between these industries and others in that respect.

Again, even if adequate data could be secured for an accurate comparison of the efficiency of a trust with that of its present single-plant competitors, this would not prove the advantage of a trust régime over a régime of separate plants. The inefficiency of the independent concerns may be due to the presence of the trust. The combination at its inception may have taken in all the larger and more efficient plants then existing. The fear of the trust, and the actual effect of its competition, fair or unfair, may have prevented the development of large competing concerns thereafter. The Standard Oil Company did produce more economically than its competitors. But who that is familiar with the outrageous tactics of the Standard toward competitors can attribute that fact wholly to the superiority of combination over competition ? Had no trust been formed in the oil industry there would certainly have developed by this time a number of large separate concerns, each with a considerable degree of integration, and with efficiency at least not greatly inferior to that of the Standard Oil Company.

In a few industries, — the steel industry, for example, — there are today comparatively large single-plant concerns standing side by side with combinations. Comparisons between them and the combinations with respect to efficiency would be fair. It is unfortunate that the Bureau of Corporations, in its desire to protect the privacy of business, was unable to present the information which it possessed about the steel industry in such a way as to permit comparisons of this character. In can only be said that its report discloses wide variations in cost of production among the individual plants of the Steel Corporation itself. It is more than probable that some of the independent concerns are superior in efficiency to the less efficient plants of the Steel Corporation, and quite likely that they compare favorably even with the most efficient of those plants. Such concerns as Jones & Laughlin, the Lackawanna Steel Company, and the Cambria Steel Company are not weaklings. They have many millions of capital and a great output. They practise integration of related stages of production to a large extent. Their plants are largely new and up to date. The Lackawanna Steel Company at Buffalo preceded the Steel Corporation in the extensive use of the by-product coke oven, one of the most important of the modern forms of economy in the steel industry. Blast furnaces of Jones & Laughlin are among the record-holders for size and efficiency.

Finally, it is obviously very difficult to judge of the advantages of combination in production and marketing by comparing the business of combinations with that of single plants in other industries. The differences in the subject matter of production and in the conditions would in most cases render such comparisons of little value.

In view of these difficulties, it is certain that detailed investigations regarding the relative efficiency of trusts and single plants, even if they covered the entire field of industry, would result only in disagreement among the people as to the conclusions to be drawn. It would probably be proved clearly enough that certain particular trusts were highly efficient. We might convince ourselves, not only that they were more efficient than the best of the predecessor concerns, or than the best of the present competing concerns, but also that they were more efficient even than such individual plants as might have come into existence in the absence of combination. In other industries, however, no such demonstration would be possible. The investigations would still leave doubt as to whether the trust in general was superior in efficiency to the separate plant.

But suppose, for purposes of argument, it should be demonstrated that in general the trust was more efficient than the individual plant. We should still have failed to show the superiority of the trust over the less extensive combination having no possibility of monopolistic power. That question could scarcely be attacked at all by statistical investigation of present or past conditions.

The basis for comparisons does not exist. In very few industries did combination on a limited scale precede monopolistic combination on a large scale. In still fewer industries have there existed, side by side, a combination controlling the greater part of the business and another combination or combinations having only a minor fraction of the business. Comparison between the trust in one industry and the smaller combination in another industry would usually lead to no definite conclusions.

The fact is that we have had comparatively little experience with combinations other than trusts and pools of a more or less monopolistic character. If the desire to secure increased efficiency had been the only motive of business men in forming combinations, we might have witnessed a large number of combinations having no controlling proportion of the business in their respective fields. But since the main object was to suppress competition, combinations of a more comprehensive character sprang at once out of the régime of separate plants.

There is no objection to further investigation regarding trust efficiency, provided it is not made an excuse for deferring action as to the dissolution of trusts. A wide-reaching investigation of trust efficiency would require not less than ten years. Every year that trusts are permitted to continue renders it more difficult to restore competition among their constituent concerns. The officers and managers year by year become more accustomed to working together; the organization year by year becomes more welded into an inseparable unit. The shock to business from breaking up combinations also will become more severe the longer it is deferred.

Since there are thus no adequate existing data on which to base conclusions as to the advantages of trusts from the standpoint of efficiency, we are forced to fall back upon general reasoning. The theoretical advantages claimed for the trusts by their defenders naturally fall into three groups, — those attributable to mere magnitude, those attributable to combination of separate plants, and those attributable to the elimination of competition. The failure to make this obvious classification is the source of much fallacious thinking. Only advantages of the third class can properly be put forward as directly proving the desirability of trusts that possess a controlling proportion of the industry in which they are engaged.

The following are some of the advantages claimed for trusts which, so far as they exist at all, exist solely by reason of the magnitude of their business.

1. Command of the largest and most efficient units of production, — buildings, power plants and machinery.

2. Command of large liquid capital and credit, enabling the concern to meet emergencies and to take advantage of special opportunities.

3. Command of superior administrative and technical ability.

4. Economy in the purchase of raw material and supplies in large quantities.

5. Distribution of administrative and other overhead expenses and of selling and advertising expenses over a large output, thus reducing unit costs.

6. Practicability of introducing efficient accounting systems too expensive for smaller concerns.

Any concern, if sufficiently large, can possess all such advantages. Magnitude of operation is purely a relative term. In minor industries, only a concern which has the greater part of the entire business can be considered large. In great industries the concern which has only a small fraction of the business may possess millions of capital, a vast plant and an army of employees. No one would think of denying that large scale operation has advantages over small scale operation. It does not follow that an industrial combination controlling the major part of a business will, by reason of size alone, be more efficient than a less extensive combination or even than a single large plant. Efficiency does not increase proportionately with size. It has been learned by the experience of business men that when the individual plant passes beyond a certain size, it ceases to gain in efficiency. The same causes which make this true of the individual plant apply to the combination of plants as well. There may be advantages from combination as such or from monopoly as such, but the advantages of mere magnitude have their limits. Moreover, when size passes beyond a certain point, it may even lessen efficiency. The unwieldiness of a vast organization, the difficulty of securing coöperation among its parts, the impossibility of personal oversight by the master mind, — these are disadvantages of excessive magnitude.

There may be some industries in which, from the standpoint of magnitude alone, the greatest efficiency would lie in a concern controlling virtually the entire business. There is little ground for believing that this is the case in the great majority of industries. At any rate it is utterly impossible, by general reasoning or by statistical investigation, to prove that it is so. Indeed, it would seem that in most industries a concern having even as much as half of the total business would, in respect to those elements of efficiency now under consideration, have no superiority over a somewhat smaller concern.

Another set of advantages claimed for trusts rests upon the fact of combination as such. These supposed advantages result from the assemblage of separate plants under a single control. They are not dependent on the elimination of competition. Among these are the following:

1. Use in all plants of the best methods and devices discovered in any one plant, comparative cost accounting rendering it possible to determine which are, in fact, the best.

2. Rivalry between the managers of different plants, stimulated by comparative cost accounts and other comparative data.

3. Saving in cross freights by shipping from the plant nearest to the desired destination.

4. Integration of industry — that is, the conduct of successive or related processes under a single management.

Combination undoubtedly does have its advantages. But combination, like magnitude, is a relative matter. In a minor industry a combination of even a few plants may mean the bringing together of the larger proportion of the business. In another industry a combination including a considerable number of plants may have but a fraction of the total business. Any combination of plants, however few, can obtain the advantages specified in some degree. Just as economies of magnitude do not increase proportionately with magnitude, so economies of combination do not increase proportionally with the number of plants combined. There is a limit beyond which the addition of plants brings no further economy. Just where the limit is can be proved neither by abstract reasoning nor by statistical investigation. It is different in different industries. There is little reason to believe that in most industries a combination controlling the entire business would be appreciably superior, with respect to the elements of efficiency above mentioned, to a combination having a minor fraction of the business.

Take, for example, the matter of cross freights. In some industries freights are not an important element of expense. In others the location of materials, or of consuming markets, or like conditions, make it impossible to locate plants with a view to saving freight either on materials or products. There are, however, a good many industries in which scattered plants competing with one another incur much needless expense in transportation. In such industries a combination by shipping from the nearest plant could effect material savings. It does not follow that a combination of all the plants in the country could save more than a combination of a moderate number of well distributed plants.

Where an industry derives peculiar advantages from the integration of successive and related processes, combination on a large scale may be essential to the full realization of economies of this character. If in a single one of the related branches of business the greatest efficiency requires the handling of a large part of the total business by a single organization, than it may be advantageous for the combination to conduct other branches of the business on a corresponding scale. There are, however, few, if any, important industries in which successful integration requires the control of the major part of the business by a single combination. In a good many instances a concern that has not more than a single plant engaged in each of the different stages of production has been able to secure an efficiency at least closely comparable with that of a wide-reaching combination. This is the case, for example, with several independent concerns in the steel industry and even with some of the recently developed independent concerns in the oil industry.

There is another economy sometimes claimed for the combination of separate plants, namely, that it is able to close down the inefficient plants and concentrate business in the largest and most modern. This, however, is not an advantage to the public. No combination, unless with monopolistic intent, would take in inefficient plants. The fact that a good many trusts have, shortly after their organization, dismantled numerous plants is proof simply of their monopolistic purpose. Under a régime of competition the inefficient plant will in due time be forced out of business and the public will no longer be burdened with supporting it. When a combination takes in an inefficient plant and dismantles it, the public pays the bill, provided the combination succeeds in obtaining a sufficient degree of monopoly power. The combination either charges prices high enough to enable it to write off the cost of such a plant out of its profits, or that cost is permanently represented by securities on which dividends are expected to be paid. A combination which takes in a limited number of selected, efficient plants is in this respect far more conducive to economy than a monopolistic combination.

It thus appears probable that most of the economies claimed for the trusts could, in many if not all industries, be secured in approximately equal measure without permitting combinations sufficiently comprehensive to possess any approach to monopoly power. There remain those alleged economies of trusts which arise not from mere magnitude or from mere assembling of separate plants, but from the elimination of competition. These require more thoro consideration. They are few, namely:

1. Prevention of needless duplication of plants.

2. Elimination of that part of the cost of selling goods which results from the effort to secure business at the expense of competitors.

3. Elimination of waste due to irregularity of operation, and of the losses of so-called destructive competition.

Let us take these up in order:

1. It is contended that competition leads to excessive investment of capital, to the erection of plants with a capacity in excess of the needs of the country. This is true only in a very limited degree of ordinary mining, manufacturing, and commercial business. Such business differs radically from the so-called industries of increasing returns, such as transportation. In order that there shall be any rail transportation between two points, it is necessary to build a track which may have more than capacity enough for all the traffic. Under such conditions, the one railroad can increase its business without corresponding new investment. In fact, up to a certain limit, even the operating expenses of a railroad do not increase proportionately with volume of business. The building of a second railroad under the conditions mentioned would mean unnecessary duplication of capital and perhaps also of the operating expenses.

In the case of the ordinary manufacturing industries it seldom happens that a single plant, however large, can supply the entire demand of the territory to which it has natural access. The construction of a second plant usually does not mean needless duplication of investment. The aggregate capacity of all plants is not likely to exceed materially the demand in times of prosperity. The desire of each competitor to be ready to get as large a share of the trade as possible may lead to some excess in plant capacity, but not to a great excess. Moreover, in manufacturing industries, even if there be some excess of plant capacity, operating expenses are not likely to be materially augmented. The plant working at less than full capacity can lessen its force more or less proportionately. Operating expenses vary fairly closely with output.

It must not be forgotten that the great majority of the industries of the country are steadily and rapidly growing. In industries where trusts are powerful, as well as in other industries, additional plant capacity is constantly being constructed, and additional working force taken on. Even if it were not for the growth of demand, the improvements in methods of production would necessitate the construction of new plants. The older and less efficient plants in a manufacturing industry ought not to be taken into account in judging the relation of plant capacity to demand.

The reasoning as to duplication of plant capacity which applies to manufacturing industries applies as well to mining and to mercantile business. There are a few manufacturing industries in which it is customary for the manufacturer to conduct also some special form of transportation. Ecomony in such transportation may demand that duplication of plant be avoided, — that there be monopolistic operation. If the transportation business cannot be divorced from the manufacture, or subjected to separate regulation, monopolistic operation of the manufacturing business as well may be unavoidable or at least advantageous. For example, the Standard Oil Company and other leading refiners of petroleum operate pipe-lines for transporting crude oil and also tank cars and tank wagons for delivering refined products. Needless duplication of plant and of operating expenses may be involved in competition in these two branches of the oil industry. Unless they can be divorced from the refining business proper, it may prove necessary to tolerate monopoly in petroleum refining. It has been proposed to require the owners of pipe-lines, be they refiners or others, to transport oil as common carriers at reasonable charges to be fixed by the government. There are serious technical difficulties in the way, but it is probable that they could be overcome by special methods of government regulation. Whether it would be possible to manage the tank-wagon delivery business in a similar way is more doubtful. Were it not for the extraordinary difficulty of regulating the prices of refined petroleum products, arising from the fact of joint cost, a simpler way of avoiding the evils of monopoly in the oil industry might be through such regulation of prices. Regulation of profits may be the most feasible plan of meeting the situation.

The Steel Corporation is also engaged in transportation. It operates railroads which to a large extent are patronized by its competitors, and it operates steamships. To require the Steel Corporation to divest itself of its railroads, — at least the more important lines which competitors may have occasion to use, — would not materially lessen the efficiency of the integration secured by that corporation. Nor would there be any serious difficulty in effectively regulating the charges of such railroads if left in the control of the Steel Corporation. At any rate, the element of transportation in the steel industry is not a factor necessitating or justifying a combination of steel manufacturing plants of sufficient size to possess any approach to monopoly power.

2. It is contended further that competition means large waste in selling expenses, due to the endeavor of business concerns to wrest trade from one another through solicitation and advertising. This is doubtless true in some industries, but it is by no means equally true in all. Where the products of an industry are standard in character, are in steady demand, and are marketed through large middlemen or to large individual consumers, even the most vigorous competition in pushing the sale of goods involves no very great expense. In the case of certain other industries, heavy selling and advertising expenses are considered necessary by business men merely for the purpose of stimulating demand and regardless of competition. Concerns which have virtually a monopoly often spend great sums in advertising their wares. However, it must be admitted that in a good many industries competition in selling does mean some economic waste. The advantage of eliminating such waste can properly be set against the disadvantages of monopolistic control.

However, needless expense in selling goods is likely sooner or later to be reduced by informal understandings not amounting to monopolistic agreements. As the competing concerns become larger and more efficient in production, their managers are likely to see the absurdity of trying to get all the trade away from one another.

3. Finally, it is contended that uncontrolled competition results in irregularity of consumption and consequently in irregularity of the operation of plants, which tends to increase costs as well as to injure the working classes and to disturb business generally. The most common illustration used to support this contention is that of the steel industry. It is urged that when by reason of active competition, prices are particularly low, the consumers of iron and steel and their cruder products buy excessive quantities and so discount their future needs as subsequently to result in very light demand. The plants in the industry, after being worked to their utmost capacity, may have to drop a large part of their force or even close altogether. Such irregularity in production is uneconomical. It has been maintained that the greater steadiness of prices since the organization of the United States Steel Corporation not only has tended to cheapen production but has been beneficial to consumers and to business generally.

It may well be questioned whether competition is as important a factor in causing irregularity of consumption of steel products as is sometimes supposed. The consumption of many of the more important products of iron and steel is necessarily variable. Those products are used primarily in the creation of new capital goods. The desire of men to invest in new capital goods varies greatly with the general conditions of prosperity or depression in business. The policy of the Steel Corporation in recent years has had less to do with the steadiness of demand for steel than the relatively continuous prosperity of the country. This is evidenced by the demoralization of prices during the last year or so.

If it were possible for trusts, when subjected to strict regulation by the government, to adjust supply accurately to demand, and to cause demand itself to be more steady, that fact would constitute an argument of considerable force in behalf of the policy of permitting trusts to exist subject to regulation. As already suggested, however, the task of the government in regulating prices for an industry subject to variable demand would be extraordinarily difficult. The efforts at doing so would probably prove far from successful in bringing about steadiness of production.

The argument with regard to the effect of competition in causing irregularity of consumption and of production is often extended further. It is urged that competition in modern industry tends to become so fierce as to destroy capital. So-called destructive competition, it is claimed, may bring even the most efficient concerns to bankruptcy. Such a result not only injures investors, but at least sometimes means actual waste of capital, and therefore, in the long run, injures consumers as well. Indeed, some believe that pools, tho possessing few advantages with respect to efficiency of production in other respects, are justifiable as means of preventing the losses of destructive competition.

The subject of destructive competition has been discussed in the second chapter with reference to its influence in driving concerns into combination. It was there shown that, in the great majority of manufacturing industries, competition is not likely to become as fierce as in transportation industries. The principle of increasing returns, which tends peculiarly to cause bitter competition, has comparatively little application in manufactures. The concern which finds current business unprofitable usually restricts its output or stops it altogether, looking to the time when the increase of demand will again render the business of the plant profitable. It does not go on cutting prices until forced into bankruptcy.

Against these alleged advantages of monopolistic combination must be set the tendency of monopoly to lessen efficiency and retard industrial progress. It is generally recognized that the possession of a monopoly tends strongly toward stagnation. Competition is a powerful spur to efficiency. The competitor who would not go to the wall must be ever on the alert. Inventions of machinery and improvements in methods are essential to successful competition. Marked as has been the progress in the railroad business of the United States, there is much reason to believe that American railroads have made less progress during the last decade or two than most American manufacturing industries, and that this is due to the comparative absence of competition in the railroad business during recent years. The relative unprogressiveness of the largely monopolized telegraph business in this country, at least till recently, has often been commented on.

It can scarcely be proved that any of the leading trusts have been particularly lacking in progressiveness, that they have actually made fewer improvements in methods than have been made in industries where competition was active. Comparisons on this point are virtually impossible. But the trusts have thus far been on the defensive both against potential competition and against public criticism. This defensive position has made them look closely to efficiency. Should the policy of permitting monopolistic combinations be adopted, there would be danger that the absence of competitive pressure would more than counterbalance any possible advantages from the elimination of competition.

Regulated monopoly is likely to be even less efficient than unregulated monopoly. The trust, if unrestricted in prices and profits, has at least a motive to do business as cheaply as possible. When, however, the trust anticipates that every reduction in costs may mean a reduction in prices, that profits resulting from increased efficiency may be wholly or largely taken from it by government regulation, even this motive tends to disappear. In the case of public service corporations various methods have been pursued, with more or less success, for securing a division of the advantages of increased efficiency between the public and the monopoly. Should the government enter upon the policy of regulating the prices and the profits of trusts, similar methods would have to be followed as far as possible. Because of the multifarious character of the different industries, however, it would be much harder to apply these methods successfully to trusts than to the limited number of public service enterprises.

Let us now bring together summarily the results of this discussion of the trust problem. We have tried to show that unregulated combination is dangerous to the public welfare. Even if they could be deprived of the weapons of unfair competition or of the advantages of natural monopoly, — a thing by no means easy, — trusts and pools would still probably possess a material degree of monopolistic power. It would be a dangerous experiment to remove the ban of the law from them without substituting effective machinery for regulation.

We have sought to show further that it is feasible to prevent by law the more formal types of combinations and of contracts in restraint of trade. It may be impossible wholly to prevent informal understandings which in some degree restrict competition. These informal understandings, however, are far less effective in maintaining monopoly prices and charges than formal combinations such as pools and trusts.

It was pointed out that the difficulties of government regulation are exceedingly great. The policy of permitting trusts to exist might result in the extension of trusts over almost the entire field of industry. It might also result in practically complete monopolization by each trust of its particular field. The determination of costs and of investment as a basis for the fixing of prices and profits over the multifarious field of industry would require immensely elaborate investigations and would involve extraordinarily difficult questions of judgment. Proper adjustment to the ever varying conditions of demand would be almost impossible. A vast governmental machinery for fixing prices and profits would have to be superimposed upon the machinery of private business. Government ownership on a vast scale or even complete socialism might readily be the outcome of this policy.

Finally, it has been shown that most of the alleged advantages of trusts in efficiency could probably be secured in quite as great measure through large individual plants and through smaller combinations not powerful enough to threaten monopoly. While the suppression of competition itself may tend to bring about certain economies and other advantages, the importance of these is usually over-estimated, and there must be set against them not only the grave difficulties of regulation, but the tendency of monopoly and of regulation itself to lessen efficiency.

It may be granted that the data and the reasoning throughout this discussion have been not altogether conclusive. It cannot be expected that every one will agree with the points of view here taken. The burden of proof, however, rests upon the defenders of the trusts. They ask us to permit the trusts to exist, whether with or without regulation. In this they are asking a departure from what until very recently were universally considered the proper principles of law and of economics. Their argument is certainly no more conclusive than the argument of those who would suppress trusts.

To defend big business is easy. The advantages of large scale production are obvious. To identify big business and large scale production with the trust is quite another thing. The glamor of the huge corporation with its mighty plants, its splendid organization, its thoro accounting system, its integration of related processes, must not blind us. All these are essential to progress. To get them we might even be willing to pay the high price of surrendering competition. But we must be sure that they can be secured at no lower price before we tender such a compensation, or before we even enter on a path which may ultimately necessitate that compensation.

To pass from a régime of competition to one of monopoly is easy. To return from a régime of monopoly to one of competition is immensely difficult. The American people have not yet tried out fully the possibilities of competitive industry. It would be foolish to abandon the experiment thus early in our national development. If we destroy as far as possible the trusts that now exist, if we prevent trusts and combinations from being formed, we shall soon see whether it is possible to secure real competition, and whether under competition efficiency can reach a high point. If not we can readily enough change our policy. On the other hand, to accept the trusts today is to leap in the dark. Every step in that direction is difficult to retrace. The results of an experiment with permitting trusts freely to organize and with regulating them could not be determined for such a long period of time that the trusts would meantime get a grip almost impossible to shake off. In fact, we never could satisfy ourselves by such an experiment that a trust régime was more satisfactory than a régime of competition, for we should have no fair example of the working of competition under similar conditions with which to make comparison.

Particularly weak would it be to allow the mere fear of a temporary disturbance of business to turn us from a safe permanent policy. The thoughtful man can have no patience with the complaint that the government is interfering with business or lowering the prices of securities by enforcing the anti-trust law. Suppose an industrial depression should be brought about? Is that a heavy price to pay for protecting the decades and the centuries of the future against a mighty evil? Granted that it is uncertain whether the trust régime would be a mighty evil, the mere possibility that it would prove such is enough to justify a present sacrifice to avert it.

The thoughtful opponent of trusts does not urge that, as the phrase goes, the government should "run amuck." It need not in a year or two attack every combination without due inquiry as to whether it actually possesses or threatens monopoly power, or as to the manner in which it is exercising such power as it does possess. A policy once determined upon and definitely announced may be carried out with reasonable deliberation and consideration of all interests. But it is high time that an end shall be put to all doubt of the intention of the people. Either they must proclaim their determination to maintain a régime of competition in manufactures and trade for an indefinite period to come, or they must promptly declare themselves for the policy of regulation. The safe policy for today is prohibition of trusts and other monopolistic combinations. It is the vigorous enforcement of the anti-trust laws, aided by the provision of expert administrative machinery such as the new trade commission.

Whether the ultimate policy adopted toward the trust be *laissez faire*, regulation or prohibition, we shall, in all probability, find it necessary to supplement the chosen policy by vigorous exercise of the taxing power. Taxation can take away a large part of monopoly profits and other unearned gains whether derived from trusts and pools, from railroads, from banking, from control of land and other natural resources, or from any other source.

Direct taxation of trusts and other business enterprises with a view to taking away excessive gains would encounter practically the same difficulties as regulation of prices and profits. Heavy income taxes upon individuals, particularly if progressive, are very hard to enforce. Inheritance taxes would be more feasible. Progressive inheritance taxes, even with rates such that much the greater part of the largest fortunes would be taken by the government, would, in the opinion of many thoughtful men, be neither unjust nor socially disadvantageous. They are defensible even when applied to fortunes derived from strictly legitimate business. Taxes of this sort might in some degree tend to check the accumulation of capital and to prevent the efficient captain of industry from exercising his talents to the utmost, but the effect in these directions would probably not be very marked. There might, too, be some difficulty in enforcing collection and preventing evasion, but on the whole the system would go far toward correcting that immense disparity of wealth and of opportunity which is the main source of social unrest.

CHAPTER V

THE TRUST LEGISLATION OF 1914

Two important acts relating to trusts and corporations have just been adopted by Congress. They represent the fruition of the policy laid down in the last national platform of the Democratic party. They are "administration measures." In fact, it is doubtful whether without the persistent and forceful leadership of President Wilson the conflicting views in Congress could have been harmonized and the legislation passed in addition to the other important and long-debated measures which have occupied the attention of that body.

The "administration" bills regarding trusts and corporations were introduced into Congress at the very beginning of 1914. They were under almost continuous consideration by the two houses and their committees for nine months before enactment. Many of the crudities of the original bills have been eliminated and in general the provisions as adopted are workable and understandable. In fact, if the destruction of trusts and the maintenance of competition be accepted as the proper policy, these acts must be approved for the most part as a valuable aid in carrying out that policy. The present work has sought to prove that this policy is on the whole the best for the American people.

As might be expected, there were efforts in Congress, particularly on the part of the Progressive party, to turn the trust legislation in the direction of regulation rather than prohibition. The Democrats, however, stood with practically united front for the policy of suppressing combinations and many Republicans joined with them.

The two acts are entitled respectively: "An Act to supplement existing laws against unlawful restraints and monopolies and for other purposes," and "An Act to create a federal trade commission, to define its powers and duties and for other purposes." We shall call them briefly the anti-trust act and the trade-commission act. The trade-commission bill, as it passed the House, was substantially confined to procedure, to machinery and methods for enforcing the laws. The Senate, however, inserted in this bill provisions with respect to unfair competitive methods, and these stand in the act as finally adopted, altho they more logically belong in the other act, which is chiefly concerned with prohibitions of unlawful practices.

It is perhaps needless to call attention to the fact that both these acts are, of necessity, limited to fields over which the federal government has jurisdiction. Except certain provisions on national banks, they deal exclusively with interstate and foreign commerce.

The new prohibitions and definitions of unlawful practices in the two acts fall under three main heads: (1) those relating to competitive methods; (2) those relating to methods and forms of combination in restraint of trade; and (3) those relating to mismanagement of railroads.

I. Unfair Competitive Methods

Of the provisions relating to methods of competition there are three, — as to unfair methods in general, as to price discrimination, and as to restrictive sales and leases. The first named was not in either bill as it passed the House but was added by the Senate. Being comprehensive in character it would, if broadly interpreted, have rendered unnecessary the more specific provisions of the House bill regarding competitive methods and these were accordingly struck out by the Senate. In the conference committee of the two houses, however, they were restored, and they were finally adopted, tho with considerable amendment.

Section 5 of the trade-commission act provides simply "that unfair methods of competition in commerce are hereby declared unlawful." This applies to individuals and firms as well as corporations. It adds no definitions or qualifications, leaving the determination of what constitutes unfair competition to the Trade Commission and the courts. In this respect the provision is similar to that of the interstate commerce act, which merely declares unreasonable railroad rates to be unlawful, leaving it to the Interstate Commerce Commission and the courts to determine what rates are unreasonable. In other words, Congress has established a standard and delegated to other agencies the sub-legislative power of applying or interpreting that standard.

There was much opposition to this general provision on the ground of its vagueness. It was stoutly maintained that no business man would know where he stood, what he could and what he could not do. The reply to this was that the methods of unfair competition are so numerous, so varied and so constantly changing that they cannot all be specifically set forth by Congress, and that a law which attempted to do so would require constant amendment. To avoid the well-founded objection that it would not do to punish a man for an offense indefinitely described, Congress wisely prescribed no penalties for initial violation of this section but provided a special and appropriate procedure for enforcement.

This procedure begins with action by the Federal Trade Commission, a body whose composition and other powers are more fully described later. No court can take initial jurisdiction of an alleged offense against this section of the law; no prosecuting attorney bring an indictment. The commission is not even obliged to take action. The law declares that whenever the commission has reason to believe that any person or concern is using unfair methods of competition it shall proceed, "if it shall appear to the commission that a proceeding by it in respect thereof would be to the interest of the public." The language just quoted was incorporated in the bill in the conference and was not in it as first passed by the Senate. While in a sense the clause materially weakens the law, there can be little doubt of its propriety, at least as a temporary device. In its absence the commission would be obliged to take up every case of unfair competition, however unimportant and however little it actually tended to bring about monopoly. Instances of more or less unfair competition are simply innumerable in the business world, and it is vain for the government to attempt, under present conditions, to prevent them all. The commission would find its hands full indeed if it had to take up every complaint brought before it. The interference with business which would result from a multitude of proceedings on the part of the commission would probably more than offset the good accomplished by the actual suppression of more important and serious abuses.

The commission having decided to take up a case of unfair competition must give a hearing, after which it may issue an order requiring the discontinuance of the unfair practice. This order, however, is not immediately enforceable. If the person or concern to whom it is directed fails to obey, the commission must apply to the circuit court of appeals for its enforcement. It will be recalled that a similar procedure formerly prevailed in case of the failure of a railroad to obey an order of the Interstate Commerce Commission, but by the amendment of 1906 a penalty was provided for failing to obey such an order and the railroad could escape the penalty only by taking the initiative in applying to the courts for relief. It is perhaps unfortunate that this amended procedure was not followed in the trade-commission act. The circuit court of appeals is given exclusive jurisdiction of cases relating to orders of the commission, thus avoiding the delay of appeals from lower courts.

The power of review given to the court with respect to orders of the Trade Commission is not without limits. The law provides that the findings of the commission as to the facts, if supported by testimony, shall be conclusive, tho the court, if it deems necessary, may order additional evidence to be taken before the commission. In other words, the court is supposed to confine itself to questions of law. Doubtless, however, the courts will treat the question whether a particular practice in competition is unfair or otherwise as one of law rather than of fact, and a very wide field for judge-made legislation is thus opened.

No specific penalties appear in the trade-commission act for failure to obey an order of the court confirming an order of the commission with respect to unfair competition. However, the general provision contained in the anti-trust act as to penalties for contempt of court would apply. The maximum penalty for a natural person is $1000 or six months' imprisonment.

In the anti-trust bill as it passed the House the practices of price discrimination and of restrictive sales and leases were made subject to penalties of fine and imprisonment. In the act as finally revised by the conference committee and passed these penalties were cut out, and the procedure for enforcing the prohibition of these practices was made similar to that for enforcing the general provision as to unfair methods of competition. There is this substantial difference, however, that in the anti-trust act the words "if it shall appear to the commission that a proceeding by it would be to the interest of the public" do not appear.

This elimination of penalties and other similar changes made in the conference were vigorously attacked on the floor both of House and Senate. It was charged that the "teeth" had been taken out of the bills. There is little reason to doubt, however, that even as to these more specifically defined practices it is much better, at least for the time being, that proceedings should begin only with the Trade Commission. Its expert investigation of the facts should be much more satisfactory than could be expected in an ordinary criminal prosecution. Indeed, in all probability the law will be enforced more vigorously and effectively under this procedure than it could have been in any other way. It is a great mistake to suppose that the establishment of severe penalties for statute-made offenses, not recognized as offenses by the common practice of the business world, will forthwith assure their cessation.

This comprehensive provision regarding unfair competitive methods bids fair to inaugurate a marked improvement in business practices in the United States and to do much toward checking the growth of monopoly. In a certain sense the new provision adds little to the Sherman anti-trust act. It will be recalled that that act explicitly prohibits the monopolization of interstate or foreign trade or the attempt to monopolize it. Unfair competitive practices, if carried to such a degree as to justify their suppression by government, are in most cases, if not in all, attempts to monopolize. The most significant feature of the new legislation is the expert machinery for investigating the facts and for making at least the initial determination as to what constitutes an unfair practice injurious to the public interest.

As regards price discrimination, the anti-trust bill as it passed the House provided that any person who discriminated in price between different purchasers in the same or different sections "with the purpose or intent thereby to destroy or wrongfully injure the business of a competitor" was subject to penalty. Rejected by the Senate, restored and amended in conference, the section (§ 2 of the anti-trust act) omits the words just quoted and declares such discrimination unlawful only where the effect " may be to substantially lessen competition or tend to create a monopoly." Moreover, to the unimportant and proper exceptions contained in the House bill is added the exception of discrimination " made in good faith to meet competition."

The wisdom of the first of these two changes can scarcely be doubted. The purpose of all competition, at least in a sense, is to destroy the business of competitors. Price discrimination is an all but universal practice and is not necessarily injurious or calculated to bring about a monopoly. The House bill if broadly interpreted would virtually have prohibited price discrimination altogether; it went too far. On the other hand, to permit price discrimination when made to " meet competition " may largely defeat the effectiveness of this section. The great corporation or combination that seeks to drive out a small competitor by price discrimination usually maintains that all it does is in good faith to meet competition. The Standard Oil Company, for example, may have the entire oil trade of a given town. It may be charging excesssive prices there. A competitor seeking to gain a foothold enters the town and offers oil at a somewhat lower price, but still a fair price. The Standard meets this price, perhaps goes below it. The merchants being accustomed to deal with the Standard give little patronage to the competitor, who must cut again, and so the process goes on till prices are below cost. Meantime the Standard recoups itself for reduced prices in the town in question by advancing them elsewhere; the less fortunate competitor is driven out of business. It is doubtful whether under the phraseology of the new statute such tactics could be held unlawful, altho they certainly would tend to create monopoly.

It would appear, therefore, that the section with regard to price discrimination, so far from adding to the effectiveness of the general provision as to unfair competitive methods, may actually weaken it.

The Senate, as already indicated, struck out the provision of the House bill prohibiting in general terms the practice of restrictive sales and leases. It substituted, however, a somewhat similar provision relating only to patented articles. The Senate evidently feared lest the holder of a patent might claim by reason of the patent the right to do that which if done by others would be held unfair competition. The courts had already upheld restrictive sales and leases of patented articles. In conference, however, this section of the bill was again made general in application, explicit reference being made to both patented and unpatented articles. Section 3 of the anti-trust act declares it unlawful for any person to lease or sell goods or fix a price therefor on the condition or understanding that the lessee or purchaser shall not use or deal in the goods of a competitor. In conference was added the qualification "where the effect . . . may be to substantially lessen competition or tend to create a monopoly."

Again there can be no doubt of the wisdom of this qualifying clause. It is common in many branches of business to make sales or leases subject to the condition of exclusive patronage. The practice is by no means necessarily objectionable. It is substantially akin to the practice of establishing agencies which handle goods on commission or on a salary basis, and which are not allowed to handle similar goods of other sellers. One seller has one dealer to handle his goods exclusively, another competing seller another dealer and so on. Competition instead of being restrained may be made the more effective thereby. Often this may be the only effective way of securing the distribution of the goods in a given locality. An unqualified prohibition of "tying contracts" would have been unfortunate. On the other hand, such contracts have been in some cases an important means of creating or protecting monopoly, and where that is the case they should be prohibited as the law now prohibits them.

It may be noted that there was a provision in the bill as it passed the House making it unlawful for mine operators and certain other concerns to refuse to sell their products to any responsible person. This was struck out by the Senate as of doubtful constitutionality and has not been restored.

II. New Provisions on Combinations in Restraint of Trade

We come now to consider those provisions of the new legislation which seek to clarify and extend the definitions of forbidden contracts and combinations in restraint of trade. These provisions, which are confined to the anti-trust act, relate chiefly to intercorporate stockholdings and to interlocking directorates.

If broadly interpreted, the Sherman anti-trust act without amendment could be made to reach every harmful, or potentially harmful, combination in restraint of interstate trade, however indirect its form. That act declares "every contract, combination in the form of trust or otherwise, or conspiracy in restraint of trade " to be unlawful. The language is comprehensive in the extreme. To be sure, the Supreme Court has declared that the Sherman act must be interpreted in the " light of reason "; that there may be certain contracts or combinations which restrain trade in only a reasonable manner and which Congress did not intend to make unlawful. President Taft and others have made it clear, however, that the Court did not in this statement refer to any contract or combination that would in any way injure the people, nor did it contemplate substituting its own judgment for that of Congress. Those restraints of trade which in the light of reason might be held lawful are only of a very limited class, such as were lawful at common law, and such as practically every one recognizes to be perfectly legitimate. There were members of Congress who proposed so to amend the Sherman act as to leave no discretion whatever to the courts. Practically, tho they would not have stated it in so many words, they would have had the law declare any restraint of trade, whether reasonable or unreasonable, to be unlawful. Better counsels prevailed, however, and no such provision appears in the new legislation.

The Sherman law being thus broad and comprehensive, the lawyer and the economist alike look with critical eye upon any attempt to add to its definitions. Has the new legislation strengthened our ability to prevent combinations in restraint of trade ? Has it forbidden anything which ought not to be forbidden ? Has it gone far enough, or gone too far ?

Section 7 of the anti-trust act contains the provisions on intercorporate stockholdings. It declares, first, that no corporation shall acquire directly or indirectly any part of the stock of another corporation, where the effect "may be to substantially lessen competition" between the two corporations, "or to restrain such commerce . . . or to tend to create a monopoly." A similar provision is made with regard to holding companies; no corporation may acquire stocks in two or more corporations under the conditions above set forth. Common carriers are included among the corporations covered. There are various exceptions to these broad prohibitions, but the only one of importance relates to stockholdings heretofore acquired. In other words, the act applies only to future acquisitions of stock and does not undertake to undo things already accomplished. Of course there is a clause to the effect that the act shall not make lawful anything theretofore prohibited by the anti-trust laws; intercorporate stockholdings which were unlawful under the Sherman act may still be attacked.

This section seems to add nothing of real value to the Sherman act. Moreover, if strictly construed, it prohibits that which should not be prohibited. Under the Sherman law the courts have already held intercorporate stockholdings unlawful when they result in unreasonable restraint of trade or in a tendency toward monopoly. Several of the great trust cases decided by the Supreme Court have turned on this point, — the Standard Oil case, the Tobacco case, the Northern Securities case, the Union Pacific case and others. The new law, however, prohibits the acquisition of stocks not merely where competition in *the* trade, — that is in the business concerned as a whole, — is restrained; but also where merely the competition between the particular corporations directly concerned is lessened. A lessening of the competition between two corporations may increase the competition in the branch of industry or commerce in which they are engaged. One corporation may control, say, one-tenth of a given branch and another corporation one-twentieth. The acquisition of stock in one by the other may completely destroy competition between them, but may thereby render them more efficient in competing with other concerns.

Doubtless the exercise of discretion by prosecuting authorities and courts will result in weakening the prohibitions of this section. In few cases perhaps will suits actually be brought and won by the government unless the public interest is threatened by the intercorporate stockholding. That, however, does not justify placing an economic and legal absurdity on the statute book. It is strange that Congress did not use, with respect to intercorporate stockholding, language similar to that used regarding interlocking directorates, which is far more closely guarded.

The administration anti-trust bill, as originally introduced in Congress, contained a provision with regard to interlocking directorates which, had it been enacted, would have been little less than disastrous. Virtually it prohibited the interlocking of directorates altogether, regardless of its effect. If two corporations, which together had only a small fraction of a given business, should have one common director, and if such corporations were natural competitors, the corporations would have been made subject to the penalties of the Sherman anti-trust law.

As it passed the House this absurd and drastic provision was toned down greatly, and in the Senate it was still farther shorn of claws by the omission of the penalty. In its final form the section (§ 8 of the anti-trust act) applies only to large corporations and only in cases where the elimination of competition by agreement between them would be unlawful. No person, it declares, shall, after two years from the passage of the act, be a director in any two or more corporations, any one of which has capital, surplus and undivided profits aggregating more than one million dollars, if such corporations have been theretofore competitors "so that the elimination of competition by agreement between them would constitute a violation of any of the provisions of any of the anti-trust laws." Nothing is said about community of officers or employees other than directors. Banks and common carriers are exempted from this general provision; but there are special provisions regarding banks.

If the fact that two or more corporations had common directors did actually result in restraint of competition, — not merely between the corporations concerned but in the trade generally, — the courts could and probably would have held it unlawful under the Sherman act. In several decisions in which combinations based on intercorporate stock ownership have been dissolved, the courts have prohibited the segregated parts from having common officers or directors. The new act, however, goes farther and prohibits corporations from having the same directors even tho they do as a matter of fact actively compete, provided only that an agreement between the corporations to eliminate competition would be unlawful. In effect it makes the interlocking of directors in such case conclusive evidence of combination to restrain trade. Perhaps on the whole this is wise, for there is at least some tendency to eliminate competition where even a single individual is a director in two or more potentially competitive corporations.

The importance of this legislation, however, has been greatly exaggerated by its sponsors. The real evil is not community of directors but community of stock ownership. It will be easy enough for an individual or group who hold stock in several corporations to elect different men as directors who will act in harmony. The director is but the voice of those who elect him. Dummy directors are no new thing and they will doubtless be more numerous under this act than at present.

Apparently no one seriously proposed in Congress to restrict community of stock ownership by individuals. As I have pointed out elsewhere,[1] the courts have expressly tolerated community of interest in cases where it was almost self-evident that the result must be to prevent competition. They have seemed to consider it an inalienable right of the individual to hold what stocks he pleases. The "dissolution" of trusts by distributing the stocks of subsidiary companies *pro rata* among the stockholders of a controlling company is an economic absurdity. The investigations of the Pujo committee emphasized the enormous extent and influence of community of stock interest as well as of interlocking directorates. But Congress seemed to be of the same mind as the courts with respect to the impossibility, or the unconstitutionality, of attempting to check the former. Some day our law makers will grow bolder; they will not permit any supposed right of private property to serve as a bulwark for monopoly.

[1] Pages 35 ff.

The special provisions regarding interlocking directorates of banks, as passed by the House, were struck out by the Senate on the ground that the matter could best be provided for in connection with the banking laws. These provisions were, however, restored, with some modifications, by the conference committee and enacted into law. They prohibit interlocking of directors, officers or employees among large banks, — those having deposits, capital, surplus and undivided profits aggregating more than five million dollars, — wherever located. Moreover, subject to minor exceptions, no two banks, of whatever size, in a city of more than 200,000 inhabitants may have a common director, officer or employee. Naturally Congress has not undertaken to regulate private banks or those organized under state laws, but the act does apply to relations between a national bank on the one hand and a private or state bank on the other.

This provision as to banks is not qualified by any reference to the effect of the interlocking. It is not on its face directed against monopoly or restraint of competition among banks or in other business. The constitutionality of this provision cannot be questioned, since the national banks are creatures of the federal government. As to its justice and propriety there may be some doubt, and as to its effectiveness, for the reasons already mentioned above, still more doubt. The investigations of the Pujo committee have indeed made clear the immense power of concentrated banking interests. If that power can be weakened by this new legislation, most people will welcome it, even tho the law may incidentally prevent interlocking directorates among banks where no disadvantages would result therefrom.

It may be noted that there are no direct penalties for violation of the provisions as to intercorporate stockholding and interlocking directorates. The enforcement, except in the case of banks, rests with the Federal Trade Commission by a procedure similar to that in the case of unfair competitive methods.

While, as already indicated, a good many teeth were drawn from the anti-trust bill during its progress through Congress, there remains one provision which distinctly increases the terrors of the law. Section 14 of the new act provides that whenever a corporation shall violate any of the penal provisions of any of the anti-trust laws, such violation shall be deemed to be also that of the individual directors, officers or agents who have authorized, ordered or done any of the acts constituting such violation. Upon conviction therefor any such director, officer or agent is subject to fine not exceeding $5000 or imprisonment not exceeding one year or both.

As is well known, practically no imprisonments have heretofore resulted from the enforcement of the anti-trust laws. Most of the fines in criminal cases under them have been assessed against corporations. It is true that individuals could be punished for conspiracy under the Sherman act; but this new section will probably make it somewhat easier to punish them. There is no immediate likelihood, however, that the prisons will be overcrowded with trust offenders.

The anti-trust act provides (§ 4) that any person injured in business or property by reason of the doing of anything forbidden in the anti-trust laws may sue and recover three-fold damages. This merely extends the similar provision of the Sherman act so as to cover all anti-trust laws including the new act itself.

Section 5 provides that a final judgment or decree in any suit brought by the United States under the anti-trust laws, to the effect that the defendant has violated those laws, shall be *prima facie* evidence against such defendant in any suit or proceeding brought by any other party against him or it under the same laws. The House bill would have made such judgment or decree conclusive evidence, but the words *prima facie* were substituted in the Senate. No one can seriously doubt the propriety of this new provision. It is a needless burden upon a state, or upon a person injured by a violation of the anti-trust laws, to have to prove independently that the trust laws have been violated when the matter has already been determined in a government suit.

III. Mismanagement of Railroads

The revelations of the Pujo investigation, of the New Haven investigation and of other recent investigations with reference to mismanagement of railroads and the mulcting of their stockholders have led to some drastic provisions, placed, perhaps somewhat illogically, in the new anti-trust act.

Those investigations had shown that great banks had often made unreasonable gains from the financing of railroads; that dummy construction companies and equipment concerns in which railroad officers were interested had made fat profits at the expense of the stockholders of the road. The anti-trust bill, as it passed the House, simply prohibited interlocking of directors or officers between a railroad and a concern of the kind specified with which it did business. In the

Senate, however, it was suggested that there might be cases where such relations were proper and desirable and that regulation rather than prohibition was called for. Substantially the provisions adopted by the Senate have now become law (§ 10). No common carrier may have dealings in securities or in supplies or may make contracts for construction or maintenance, to the amount of more than $50,000 in any one year, with a concern in which any director or any of certain specified officers of the railroad is interested, except under the conditions specified in the act. These conditions are, virtually, competition, publicity and supervision by the Interstate Commerce Commission. If the concern in question is the most favorable bidder under competitive bidding, the railroad may do business with it, but it must report the transactions to the Interstate Commerce Commission in detail and the commission may investigate to see whether there has been any abuse. Penalties are provided for violation of this section.

Another outcome of the recent revelations of railroad abuses is in section 9 of the anti-trust act, which declares that an officer or director of a common carrier who "embezzles, steals, abstracts or wilfully misapplies or wilfully permits to be misapplied" its money, securities or property is guilty of a felony. Such acts are, in general, already made crimes under the laws of the individual states, but it will perhaps be possible for the federal government to enforce them more effectively in the case of interstate carriers.

IV. The Federal Trade Commission

By all odds the most important feature of the new trust legislation is the creation of a Federal Trade Commission. The commission is composed of five members, appointed by the President with the advice and consent of the Senate. Not more than three may be of the same political party — a provision which is of doubtful merit, as it really recognizes party lines in the administration of that which should be looked upon as wholly outside of those lines. The term of office is seven years and the salary $10,000. The commission is in fact to be a body of similar dignity with the Interstate Commerce Commission, tho the latter has seven members.

The commission is to take over the Bureau of Corporations and the head of that bureau, Honorable Joseph E. Davies, has been appointed a member of the commission. The expert employees of the bureau will be a useful nucleus for the force of the commission. It may be noted that the special experts and examiners which the commission is authorized to employ are exempted from the classified civil service. It is a long step from a bureau of corporations headed by a single commissioner at a salary of $5000 to a board of five members, each paid twice that salary. Useful as have been the investigations of the bureau, the public has a right to expect from this great new connission results of a far more important character.

The new act contains full provisions as to the investigatory powers of the Trade Commission. In substance it gives the commission complete power to investigate the affairs of all corporations engaged in interstate or foreign commerce, except common carriers and banks. The commission and its agents have access to the books and records of corporations and may require by subpoena the production of any or all of their papers. Witnesses may also be required to appear and testify. There are the usual provisions regarding testimony tending to incriminate its giver; he may not refuse to testify on that account, but is thereafter immune from prosecution.

The investigatory powers of the commission thus far mentioned are not materially greater than those heretofore possessed by the Bureau of Corporations. But the law creating that bureau made no definite provision for annual or special reports from corporations, and the general powers of investigation conferred on it have never been assumed to empower the bureau to demand such reports. The new law, however, explicitly authorizes the Trade Commission to require annual or special reports from any corporation engaged in interstate or foreign commerce except banks and common carriers. The commission is not compelled to call for reports from every corporation; it can determine what classes of corporations or what particular corporations must report and also determine the scope and character of the information to be furnished. The commission may require the reports to be under oath.

These powers of the commission with respect to reports from corporations are approximately the same as those given to the Interstate Commerce Commission with respect to railroads. The Trade Commission, however, lacks the power possessed by the latter to prescribe systems of accounts for corporations and to prevent them from keeping other accounts. It would doubtless be premature to give the Trade Commission that power. To devise satisfactory accounting systems for the multiplicity of corporations in different lines of business would take years. Obviously the accounts cannot be uniform to any such degree as those of railroads. For this reason the reports to be required from corporations will necessarily at first be less detailed than those made by railroads, and will probably not be so reliable, even tho made in entire good faith.

The new act prescribes penalties for failure to make reports required by the commission or for making false reports. But it goes much further. Any person who wilfully makes or causes to be made any false entry in any account or record kept by a corporation is declared guilty of a misdemeanor. So too is any one who neglects or fails to make full and correct entries in such accounts and records of all facts and transactions appertaining to the business of the corporation. This certainly is a drastic provision and will have to be interpreted with reasonable liberality. Finally, penalties are prescribed for altering or falsifying any documentary evidence of a corporation or for removing it out of the jurisdiction of the United States. The salutary character of these provisions is obvious.

The information secured from the reports of corporations to the Trade Commission will not merely be of great aid to that commission itself in the exercise of its other powers, but if the more important data are published they will serve other most useful purposes. It has been a common contention that publicity alone will go far toward preventing excessive charges and other corporate abuses. The benefits of publicity in this direction have sometimes been exaggerated, but they are important. If the reports show that corporations in a given line of business are making unusually large profits competition will be the more likely to enter the field and bring down prices.

Under the new act the Trade Commission itself decides what information obtained by it, — by whatever means obtained, — shall be made public, save only that the law prohibits the commission from publishing trade secrets and names of customers. The term "trade secrets" will undoubtedly be taken to mean merely secrets as to processes of production and the like. The general language of the law seems to imply the expectation that a great deal of information secured by the commission will be made public. It is sincerely to be hoped that the Trade Commission will see fit to make public all the important information it secures through the system of reports or in other ways, just as the Interstate Commerce Commission does. It will be recalled that under the law creating the Bureau of Corporations that bureau itself has no power to determine what information secured by it shall be made public, the determination resting with the President. As a matter of fact the President, presumably at the instance of the bureau, has withheld some information regarding individual corporations which would have been of material value to the public. A few years ago sentiment in the business world was scarcely ripe for such a measure of publicity as may properly be demanded today. In fact great corporations are more and more on their own initiative adopting the policy of making full reports to the public. The injury to a business concern from the disclosure of its affairs is seldom serious, and any concern whose business is so great as to affect materially the welfare of masses of people has no right to consider itself a private institution.

Reference has already been made to the important powers of the Federal Trade Commission as to the enforcement of the new provisions of the anti-trust legislation. The general prohibition of unfair competitive methods, that of price discrimination and that of restrictive sales and leases are enforceable only through the commission. The same is true of the prohibitions with regard to intercorporate stock ownership and interlocking directorates, — except as they relate to banks and common carriers, where other federal boards have jurisdiction. This is clearly as it should be, at least for the time being. The commission through its expert investigation will be able soon to amass a great body of information regarding competitive methods and methods of combination. Such information is largely lacking at the present time. On the basis of such information the commission should develop a sounder judgment regarding these matters than could be expected of prosecuting officers or judges.

In addition to its special powers in the enforcement of the provisions mentioned, the commission is required to aid in the enforcement of the anti-trust laws generally (§ 6). On the direction of the President or either house of Congress it has the power and duty to investigate and report the facts relating to alleged violation of the anti-trust acts by any corporation. Upon the application of the attorney general it must investigate and make recommendations in order that a corporation alleged to be violating the anti-trust acts " may thereafter maintain its organization, management and conduct of business in accordance with law." It is well known that in a number of instances in recent years great corporate combinations have, without suit by the government, changed their organization or methods of business, with a view to conforming to the Sherman act. In such cases they have usually consulted the attorney general and secured his approval. Thus to readjust business without appeal to the courts is evidently desirable. It saves expense and friction. It is obvious, however, that an expert body like the Trade Commission will be in a much better position than the attorney general to suggest the proper changes in practices and in organization.

Again, the new law provides (§ 7) that the Trade Commission may be called upon for assistance and advice in connection with the actual conduct of a suit in equity brought by the government under the anti-trust acts. The court may upon the conclusion of the testimony in such a suit, if it is of the opinion that a decree should be made against the defendants, "refer said suit to the commission, as a master in chancery, to ascertain and report an appropriate form of decree therein." The court, of course, can reject such a report in whole or in part. It is very likely not only that the courts will in fact often call upon the commission but that they will usually follow its suggestions. This again is a provision of much importance. Had the recommendations of an expert body such as the Trade Commission been before the Court in connection with the dissolution of the Standard Oil Company, for example, it is scarcely conceivable that that dissolution should have taken a form so ineffective as it did. How to secure a satisfactory dissolution of a trust is an immensely difficult economic problem, rather than a legal problem. A plan must be devised which will at the same time effectively restore competition and avoid needless hardship to the owners or stockholders of the combination and undue shock to the business world.

Finally, the Trade Commission under the new law (§ 6) may on its own initiative investigate the manner in which any decree against a defendant in a suit brought by the government to restrain violation of the anti-trust acts is being carried out. Upon the application of the attorney general it is its duty to make such an investigation. At present it too often happens that when a court has ordered the dissolution of a combination, or issued some other order for the enforcement of the anti-trust laws, very little attention is given by any one to the question whether the decree is actually obeyed. The commission should be able to render a valuable service in this direction.

The Trade Commission is also directed to report to Congress from time to time its recommendations for further legislation regarding corporations, combinations and trade practices. There is every reason to believe that the commission will have a great and beneficial influence upon future legislation. If Congress had gone no farther at the present session than to create such a commission, give it powers of investigation and call upon it for recommendations regarding future action, the trust legislation would have been well worth while. The ordinary methods of inquiry on which Congress bases legislation are by no means adequate to a problem as vast and complex as the trust problem. The time is not yet ripe for the enactment by Congress of a mass of details regarding combinations, corporations and competitive methods. In fact, a good deal even of the legislation actually adopted at this session has been, as already shown, a trifle immature. It is better to proceed slowly and surely than to make blunders.

The creation of the Trade Commission is, therefore, a great forward step. All parties in Congress were alike in favoring such a commission. Public sentiment throughout the country demanded it. The trusts and corporations were in general glad to see it established. An inquiry sent out by the National Chamber of Commerce to its constituents, consisting of trade organizations throughout the country, elicited an almost unanimous recommendation of such a commission. It matters not so much what its particular powers are at the outset, or what are for the time being the provisions of law as to trusts, combinations and trade practices. The important thing is to have a body of proper dignity devoted to the expert consideration of these great problems.[1]

[1] It is not necessary here to discuss the important new provisions of the anti-trust act with reference to labor or those with reference to the use of the injunction and the procedure for contempt of court. While the latter will have some bearing on cases against trusts and corporations, their chief significance is with respect to labor cases.

APPENDIX

FEDERAL LAWS RELATING TO TRUSTS AND ALLIED MATTERS

I. Sherman Anti-trust Law

Approved July 2, 1890

An Act to protect trade and commerce against unlawful restraints and monopolies

Sec. 1. Every contract, combination in the form of trust or otherwise, or conspiracy, in restraint of trade or commerce among the several States, or with foreign nations, is hereby declared to be illegal. Every person who shall make any such contract, or engage in any such combination or conspiracy, shall be deemed guilty of a misdemeanor, and, on conviction thereof, shall be punished by fine not exceeding five thousand dollars, or by imprisonment not exceeding one year, or by both said punishments, in the discretion of the court.

Sec. 2. Every person who shall monopolize, or attempt to monopolize, or combine or conspire with any other person or persons, to monopolize any part of the trade or commerce among the several States, or with foreign nations, shall be deemed guilty of a misdemeanor, and, on conviction thereof, shall be punished by fine not exceeding five thousand dollars, or by imprisonment not exceeding one year, or by both said punishments, in the discretion of the court.

Sec. 3. Every contract, combination in form of trust or otherwise, or conspiracy, in restraint of trade or commerce in any Territory of the United States or of the District of Columbia, or in restraint of trade or commerce between any such Territory and another, or between any such Territory or Territories and any State or States or the District of Columbia, or with foreign nations, or between the District of Columbia and any State or States or foreign nations, is hereby declared illegal. Every person who shall make any such contract or engage in any such combination or conspiracy shall be deemed guilty of a misdemeanor, and, on conviction thereof, shall be punished by fine not exceeding five thousand dollars, or by imprisonment not exceeding one year, or by both said punishments, in the discretion of the court.

SEC. 4. The several [circuit courts] [1] of the United States are hereby invested with jurisdiction to prevent and restrain violations of this act; and it shall be the duty of the several district-attorneys of the United States, in their respective districts, under the direction of the Attorney-General, to institute proceedings in equity to prevent and restrain such violations. Such proceedings may be by way of petition setting forth the case and praying that such violation shall be enjoined or otherwise prohibited. When the parties complained of shall have been duly notified of such petition the court shall proceed, as soon as may be, to the hearing and determination of the case; and pending such petition and before final decree, the court may at any time make such temporary restraining order or prohibition as shall be deemed just in the premises.

SEC. 5. Whenever it shall appear to the court before which any proceeding under section four of this act may be pending, that the ends of justice require that other parties should be brought before the court, the court may cause them to be summoned, whether they reside in the district in which the court is held or not; and subpoenas to that end may be served in any district by the marshal thereof.

SEC. 6. Any property owned under any contract or by any combination or pursuant to any conspiracy (and being the subject thereof) mentioned in section one of this act, and being in the course of transportation from one State to another, or to a foreign country, shall be forfeited to the United States, and may be seized and condemned by like proceedings as those provided by law for the forfeiture, seizure, and condemnation of property imported into the United States contrary to law.

SEC. 7. Any person who shall be injured in his business or property by any other person or corporation by reason of anything forbidden or declared to be unlawful by this act may sue therefor in any [circuit court] of the United States in the district in which the defendant resides or is found, without respect to the amount in controversy, and shall recover threefold the damages by him sustained, and the costs of suit, including a reasonable attorney's fee.

SEC. 8. The word "person," or "persons," wherever used in this act shall be deemed to include corporations and associations existing under or authorized by the laws of either the United States, the laws of any of the territories, the laws of any State or the laws of any foreign country.

(26 Statutes at Large, 210.)

[1] The Circuit Courts have been abolished and their jurisdiction conferred on the district courts.

II. Anti-trust Act of 1914

Approved October 15, 1914, Chap. 212

An Act to supplement existing laws against unlawful restraints and monopolies, and for other purposes

Sec. 1. "Anti-trust laws," as used herein, includes the Act entitled "An Act to protect trade and commerce against unlawful restraints and monopolies," approved July second, eighteen hundred and ninety; sections seventy-three to seventy-seven, inclusive, of an Act entitled "An Act to reduce taxation, to provide revenue for the Government, and for other purposes," of August twenty-seventh, eighteen hundred and ninety-four; an Act entitled "An Act to amend sections seventy-three and seventy-six of the Act of August twenty-seventh, eighteen hundred and ninety-four, entitled 'An Act to reduce taxation, to provide revenue for the Government, and for other purposes,'" approved February twelfth, nineteen hundred and thirteen; and also this Act.

"Commerce," as used herein, means trade or commerce among the several States and with foreign nations, or between the District of Columbia or any Territory of the United States and any State, Territory, or foreign nation, or between any insular possessions or other places under the jurisdiction of the United States, or between any such possession or place and any State or Territory of the United States or the District of Columbia or any foreign nation, or within the District of Columbia or any Territory or any insular possession or other place under the jurisdiction of the United States: *Provided*, That nothing in this Act contained shall apply to the Philippine Islands.

The word "person" or "persons" wherever used in this Act shall be deemed to include corporations and associations existing under or authorized by the laws of either the United States, the laws of any of the Territories, the laws of any State, or the laws of any foreign country.

Sec. 2. It shall be unlawful for any person engaged in commerce, in the course of such commerce, either directly or indirectly to discriminate in price between different purchasers of commodities, which commodities are sold for use, consumption, or resale within the United States or any Territory thereof or the District of Columbia or any insular possession or other place under the jurisdiction of the United States, where the effect of such discrimination may be to substantially lessen competition or tend to create a monopoly in any line of commerce: *Provided,* That nothing herein contained shall prevent discrimination in price between purchasers of commodities on account of differences in the grade, quality, or quantity of the commodity sold, or that makes only due allowance for difference in the cost of selling or transportation, or discrimination in price in the same or different communities made in good faith to meet competition: *And provided further,* That nothing herein contained shall prevent persons engaged in selling goods, wares, or merchandise in commerce from selecting their own customers in bona fide transactions and not in restraint of trade.

Sec. 3. It shall be unlawful for any person engaged in commerce, in the course of such commerce, to lease or make a sale or contract for sale of goods, wares, merchandise, machinery, supplies or other commodities, whether patented or unpatented, for use, consumption or resale within the United States or any Territory thereof or the District of Columbia or any insular possession or other place under the jurisdiction of the United States, or fix a price charged therefor, or discount from, or rebate upon, such price, on the condition, agreement or understanding that the lessee or purchaser thereof shall not use or deal in the goods, wares, merchandise, machinery, supplies or other commodities of a competitor or competitors of the lessor or seller, where the effect of such lease, sale, or contract for sale or such condition, agreement or understanding may be to substantially lessen competition or tend to create a monopoly in any line of commerce.

Sec. 4. Any person who shall be injured in his business or property by reason of anything forbidden in the anti-trust laws may sue therefor in any district court of the United States in the district in which the defendant resides or is found or has an agent, without respect to the amount in controversy, and shall recover threefold the damages by him sustained, and the cost of suit, including a reasonable attorney's fee.

Sec. 5. A final judgment or decree hereafter rendered in any criminal prosecution or in any suit or proceeding in equity brought by or on behalf of the United States under the anti-trust laws to the effect that a defendant has violated said laws shall be prima facie evidence against such defendant in any suit or proceeding brought by any other party against such defendant under said laws as to all matters respecting which said judgment or decree would be an estoppel as between the parties thereto: *Provided,* This section shall not apply to consent judgments or decrees entered before any testimony has been taken: *Provided further,* This section shall not apply to consent judgments or decrees rendered in criminal proceedings or suits in equity, now pending, in which the taking of testimony has been commenced but has not been concluded, provided such judgments or decrees are rendered before any further testimony is taken.

Whenever any suit or proceeding in equity or criminal prosecution is instituted by the United States to prevent, restrain or punish violations of any of the anti-trust laws, the running of the statute of limitations in respect of each and every private right of action arising under said laws and based in whole or in part on any matter complained of in said suit or proceeding shall be suspended during the pendency thereof.

SEC. 6. The labor of a human being is not a commodity or article of commerce. Nothing contained in the anti-trust laws shall be construed to forbid the existence and operation of labor, agricultural, or horticultural organizations, instituted for the purposes of mutual help, and not having capital stock or conducted for profit, or to forbid or restrain individual members of such organizations from lawfully carrying out the legitimate objects thereof; nor shall such organizations, or the members thereof, be held or construed to be illegal combinations or conspiracies in restraint of trade, under the anti-trust laws.

SEC. 7. No corporation engaged in commerce shall acquire, directly or indirectly, the whole or any part of the stock or other share capital of another corporation engaged also in commerce, where the effect of such acquisition may be to substantially lessen competition between the corporation whose stock is so acquired and the corporation making the acquisition, or to restrain such commerce in any section or community, or tend to create a monopoly of any line of commerce.

No corporation shall acquire, directly or indirectly, the whole or any part of the stock or other share capital of two or more corporations engaged in commerce where the effect of such acquisition, or the use of such stock by the voting or granting of proxies or otherwise, may be to substantially lessen competition between such corporations, or any of them, whose stock or other share capital is so acquired, or to restrain such commerce in any section or community, or tend to create a monopoly of any line of commerce.

This section shall not apply to corporations purchasing such stock solely for investment and not using the same by voting or otherwise to bring about, or in attempting to bring about, the substantial lessening of competition. Nor shall anything contained in this section prevent a corporation engaged in commerce from causing the formation of subsidiary corporations for the actual carrying on of their immediate lawful business, or the natural and legitimate branches or extensions thereof, or from owning and holding all or a part of the stock of such subsidiary corporations, when the effect of such formation is not to substantially lessen competition.

Nor shall anything herein contained be construed to prohibit any common carrier subject to the laws to regulate commerce from aiding in the construction of branches or short lines so located as to become feeders to the main line of the company so aiding in such construction or from acquiring or owning all or any part of the stock of such branch lines, nor to prevent any such common carrier from acquiring and owning all or any part of the stock of a branch or short line constructed by an independent company where there is no substantial competition between the company owning the branch line so constructed and the company owning the main line acquiring the property or an interest therein, nor to prevent such common carrier from extending any of its lines through the medium of the acquisition of stock or otherwise of any other such common carrier where there is no substantial competition between the company extending its lines and the company whose stock, property, or an interest therein is so acquired.

Nothing contained in this section shall be held to affect or impair any right heretofore legally acquired: *Provided*, That nothing in this section shall be held or construed to authorize or make lawful anything heretofore prohibited or made illegal by the anti-trust laws, nor to exempt any person from the penal provisions thereof or the civil remedies therein provided.

SEC. 8. From and after two years from the date of the approval of this Act no person shall at the same time be a director or other officer or employee of more than one bank, banking association or trust company, organized or operating under the laws of the United States, either of which has deposits, capital, surplus, and undivided profits aggregating more than $5,000,000; and no private banker or person who is a director in any bank or trust company, organized and operating under the laws of a State, having deposits, capital, surplus, and undivided profits aggregating more than $5,000,000, shall be eligible to be a director in any bank or banking association organized or operating under the laws of the United States. The eligibility of a director, officer, or employee under the foregoing provisions shall be determined by the average amount of deposits, capital, surplus, and undivided profits as shown in the official statements of such bank, banking association, or trust company filed as provided by law during the fiscal year next preceding the date set for the annual election of directors, and when a director, officer, or employee has been elected or selected in accordance with the provisions of this Act it shall be lawful for him to continue as such for one year thereafter under said election or employment.

No bank, banking association or trust company, organized or operating under the laws of the United States, in any city or incorporated town or village of more than two hundred thousand inhabitants, as shown by the last preceding decennial census of the United States, shall have as a director or other officer or employee any private banker, or any director or other officer or employee of any other bank, banking association or trust company located in the same place: *Provided*, That nothing in this section shall apply to mutual savings banks not having a capital stock represented by shares: *Provided further*, That a director or other officer or employee of such bank, banking association, or trust company may be a director or other officer or employee of not more than one other bank or trust company organized under the laws of the United States or any State where the entire capital stock of one is owned by stockholders in the other: *And provided further*, That nothing contained in this section shall forbid a director of class A of a Federal reserve bank, as defined in the Federal Reserve Act from being an officer or director or both an officer and director in one member bank.

That from and after two years from the date of the approval of this Act no person at the same time shall be a director in any two or more corporations, any one of which has capital, surplus, and undivided profits aggregating more than $1,000,000, engaged in whole or in part in commerce, other than banks, banking associations, trust companies and common carriers subject to the Act to regulate commerce, approved February fourth, eighteen hundred and eighty-seven, if such corporations are or shall have been theretofore, by virtue of their business and location of operation, competitors, so that the elimination of competition by agreement between them would constitute a violation of any of the provisions of any of the anti-trust laws. The eligibility of a director under the foregoing provision shall be determined by the aggregate amount of the capital, surplus, and undivided profits, exclusive of dividends declared but not paid to stockholders, at the end of the fiscal year of said corporation next preceding the election of directors, and when a director has been elected in accordance with the provisions of this Act it shall be lawful for him to continue as such for one year thereafter.

When any person elected or chosen as a director or officer or selected as an employee of any bank or other corporation subject to the provisions of this Act is eligible at the time of his election or selection to act for such bank or other corporation in such capacity his eligibility to act in such capacity shall not be affected and he shall not become or be deemed amenable to any of the provisions hereof by reason of any change in the affairs of such bank or other corporation from whatsoever cause, whether specifically excepted by any of the provisions hereof or not, until the expiration of one year from the date of his election or employment.

Sec. 9. Every president, director, officer or manager of any firm, association or corporation engaged in commerce as a common carrier, who embezzles, steals, abstracts or willfully misapplies, or willfully permits to be misapplied, any of the moneys, funds, credits, securities, property or assets of such firm, association or corporation, arising or accruing from, or used in, such commerce, in whole or in part, or willfully or knowingly converts the same to his own use or to the use of another, shall be deemed guilty of a felony and upon conviction shall be fined not less than $500 or confined in the penitentiary not less than one year nor more than ten years, or both, in the discretion of the court.

Prosecutions hereunder may be in the district court of the United States for the district wherein the offense may have been committed.

That nothing in this section shall be held to take away or impair the jurisdiction of the courts of the several States under the laws thereof; and a judgment of conviction or acquittal on the merits under the laws of any State shall be a bar to any prosecution hereunder for the same act or acts.

Sec. 10. After two years from the approval of this Act no common carrier engaged in commerce shall have any dealings in securities, supplies or other articles of commerce, or shall make or have any contracts for construction or maintenance of any kind, to the amount of more than $50,000, in the aggregate, in any one year, with another corporation, firm, partnership or association when the said common carrier shall have upon its board of directors or as its president, manager or as its purchasing or selling officer, or agent in the particular transaction, any person who is at the same time a director, manager, or purchasing or selling officer of, or who has any substantial interest in, such other corporation, firm, partnership or association, unless and except such purchases shall be made from, or such dealings shall be with, the bidder whose bid is the most favorable to such common carrier, to be ascertained by competitive bidding under regulations to be prescribed by rule or otherwise by the Interstate Commerce Commission. No bid shall be received unless the name and address of the bidder or the names and addresses of the officers, directors and general managers thereof, if the bidder be a corporation, or of the members, if it be a partnership or firm, be given with the bid.

Any person who shall, directly or indirectly, do or attempt to do anything to prevent any one from bidding or shall do any act to prevent free and fair competition among the bidders or those desiring to bid shall be punished as prescribed in this section in the case of an officer or director.

Every such common carrier having any such transactions or making any such purchases shall within thirty days after making the same file with the Interstate Commerce Commission a full and detailed statement of the transaction showing the manner of the competitive bidding, who were the bidders, and the names and addresses of the directors and officers of the corporations and the members of the firm or partnership bidding; and whenever the said commission shall, after investigation or hearing, have reason to believe that the law has been violated in and about the said purchases or transactions it shall transmit all papers and documents and its own views or findings regarding the transaction to the Attorney-General.

If any common carrier shall violate this section it shall be fined not exceeding $25,000; and every such director, agent, manager or officer thereof who shall have knowingly voted for or directed the act constituting such violation or who shall have aided or abetted in such violation shall be deemed guilty of a misdemeanor and shall be fined not exceeding $5,000, or confined in jail not exceeding one year, or both, in the discretion of the court.

SEC. 11. Authority to enforce compliance with sections two, three, seven and eight of this Act by the persons respectively subject thereto is hereby vested: in the Interstate Commerce Commission where applicable to common carriers, in the Federal Reserve Board where applicable to banks, banking associations and trust companies, and in the Federal Trade Commission where applicable to all other character of commerce, to be exercised as follows:

Whenever the commission or board vested with jurisdiction thereof shall have reason to believe that any person is violating or has violated any of the provisions of sections two, three, seven and eight of this Act, it shall issue and serve upon such person a complaint stating its charges in that respect, and containing a notice of a hearing upon a day and at a place therein fixed at least thirty days after the service of said complaint. The person so complained of shall have the right to appear at the place and time so fixed and show cause why an order should not be entered by the commission or board requiring such person to cease and desist from the violation of the law so charged in said complaint. Any person may make application, and upon good cause shown may be allowed by the commission or board, to intervene and appear in said proceeding by counsel or in person. The testimony in any such proceeding shall be reduced to writing and filed in the office of the commission or board. If upon such hearing the commission or board, as the case may be, shall be of the opinion that any of the provisions of said sections have been or are being violated, it shall make a report in writing in which it shall state its findings as to the facts, and shall issue and cause to be served on such person an order requiring such person to cease and desist from such violations, and divest itself of the stock held or rid itself of the directors chosen contrary to the provisions of sections seven and eight of this Act, if any there be, in the manner and within the time fixed by said order. Until a transcript of the record in such hearing shall have been filed in a circuit court of appeals of the United States, as hereinafter provided, the commission or board may at any time, upon such notice and in such manner as it shall deem proper, modify or set aside, in whole or in part, any report or any order made or issued by it under this section.

If such person fails or neglects to obey such order of the commission or board while the same is in effect, the commission or board may apply to the circuit court of appeals of the United States, within any circuit where the violation complained of was or is being committed or where such person resides or carries on business, for the enforcement of its order, and shall certify and file with its application a transcript of the entire record in the proceeding, including all the testimony taken and the report and order of the commission or board. Upon such filing of the application and transcript the court shall cause notice thereof to be served upon such person and thereupon shall have jurisdiction of the proceeding and of the question determined therein, and shall have power to make and enter upon the pleadings, testimony, and proceedings set forth in such transcript a decree affirming, modifying, or setting aside the order of the commission or board. The findings of the commission or board as to the facts, if supported by testimony, shall be conclusive. If either party shall apply to the court for leave to adduce additional evidence, and shall show to the satisfaction of the court that such additional evidence is material and that there were reasonable grounds for the failure to adduce such evidence in the proceeding before the commission or board, the court may order such additional evidence to be taken before the commission or board and to be adduced upon the hearing in such manner and upon such terms and conditions as to the court may seem proper. The commission or board may modify its findings as to the facts, or make new findings, by reason of the additional evidence so taken, and it shall file such modified or new findings, which, if supported by testimony, shall be conclusive, and its recommendation, if any, for the modification or setting aside of its original order, with the return of such additional evidence. The judgment and decree of the court shall be final, except that the same shall be subject to review by the Supreme Court upon certiorari as provided in section two hundred and forty of the Judicial Code.

Any party required by such order of the commission or board to cease and desist from a violation charged may obtain a review of such order in said circuit court of appeals by filing in the court a written petition praying that the order of the commission or board be set aside. A copy of such petition shall be forthwith served upon the commission or board, and thereupon the commission or board forthwith shall certify and file in the court a transcript of the record as hereinbefore provided. Upon the filing of the transcript the court shall have the same jurisdiction to affirm, set aside, or modify the order of the commission or board as in the case of an application by the commission or board for the enforcement of its order, and the findings of the commission or board as to the facts, if supported by testimony, shall in like manner be conclusive.

The jurisdiction of the circuit court of appeals of the United States to enforce, set aside, or modify orders of the commission or board shall be exclusive.

Such proceedings in the circuit court of appeals shall be given precedence over other cases pending therein, and shall be in every way expedited. No order of the commission or board or the judgment of the court to enforce the same shall in any wise relieve or absolve any person from any liability under the anti-trust Acts.

Complaints, orders, and other processes of the commission or board under this section may be served by any one duly authorized by the commission or board, either (*a*) by delivering a copy thereof to the person to be served, or to a member of the partnership to be served, or to the president, secretary, or other executive officer or a director of the corporation to be served; or (*b*) by leaving a copy thereof at the principal office or place of business of such person; or (*c*) by registering and mailing a copy thereof addressed to such person at his principal office or place of business. The verified return by the person so serving said complaint, order, or other process setting forth the manner of said service shall be proof of the same, and the return post-office receipt for said complaint, order, or other process registered and mailed as aforesaid shall be proof of the service of the same.

SEC. 12. Any suit, action, or proceeding under the anti-trust laws against a corporation may be brought not only in the judicial district whereof it is an inhabitant, but also in any district wherein it may be found or transacts business; and all process in such cases may be served in the district of which it is an inhabitant, or wherever it may be found.

SEC. 13. In any suit, action, or proceeding brought by or on behalf of the United States subpoenas for witnesses who are required to attend a court of the United States in any judicial district in any case, civil or criminal, arising under the anti-trust laws may run into any other district: *Provided*, That in civil cases no writ of subpoena shall issue for witnesses living out of the district in which the court is held at a greater distance than one hundred miles from the place of holding the same without the permission of the trial court being first had upon proper application and cause shown.

SEC. 14. Whenever a corporation shall violate any of the penal provisions of the anti-trust laws, such violation shall be deemed to be also that of the individual directors, officers, or agents of such corporation who shall have authorized, ordered, or done any of the acts constituting in whole or in part such violation, and such violation shall be deemed a misdemeanor, and upon conviction therefor of any such director, officer, or agent he shall be punished by a fine of not exceeding $5,000 or by imprisonment for not exceeding one year, or by both, in the discretion of the court.

SEC. 15. The several district courts of the United States are hereby invested with jurisdiction to prevent and restrain violations of this Act, and it shall be the duty of the several district attorneys of the United States, in their respective districts, under the direction of the Attorney-General, to institute proceedings in equity to prevent and restrain such violations. Such proceedings may be by way of petition setting forth the case and praying that such violation shall be enjoined or otherwise prohibited. When the parties complained of shall have been duly notified of such petition, the court shall proceed, as soon as may be, to the hearing and determination of the case; and pending such petition, and before final decree, the court may at any time make such temporary restraining order or prohibition as shall be deemed just in the premises. Whenever it shall appear to the court before which any such proceeding may be pending that the ends of justice require that other parties should be brought before the court, the court may cause them to be summoned whether they reside in the district in which the court is held or not, and subpoenas to that end may be served in any district by the marshal thereof.

SEC. 16. That any person, firm, corporation, or association shall be entitled to sue for and have injunctive relief, in any court of the United States having jurisdiction over the parties, against threatened loss or damage by a violation of the anti-trust laws, including sections two, three, seven and eight of this Act, when and under the same conditions and principles as injunctive relief against threatened conduct that will cause loss or damage is granted by courts of equity, under the rules governing such proceedings, and upon the execution of proper bond against damages for an injunction improvidently granted and a showing that the danger of irreparable loss or damage is immediate, a preliminary injunction may issue: *Provided*, That nothing herein contained shall be construed to entitle any person, firm, corporation, or association, except the United States, to bring suit in equity for injunctive relief against any common carrier subject to the provisions of the Act to regulate commerce, approved February fourth, eighteen hundred and eighty-seven, in respect of any matter subject to the regulation, supervision, or other jurisdiction of the Interstate Commerce Commission.

Sec. 17. No preliminary injunction shall be issued without notice to the opposite party.

No temporary restraining order shall be granted without notice to the opposite party unless it shall clearly appear from specific facts shown by affidavit or by the verified bill that immediate and irreparable injury, loss, or damage will result to the applicant before notice can be served and a hearing had thereon. Every such temporary restraining order shall be indorsed with the date and hour of issuance, shall be forthwith filed in the clerk's office and entered of record, shall define the injury and state why it is irreparable and why the order was granted without notice, and shall by its terms expire within such time after entry, not to exceed ten days, as the court or judge may fix, unless within the time so fixed the order is extended for a like period for good cause shown, and the reasons for such extension shall be entered of record. In case a temporary restraining order shall be granted without notice in the contingency specified, the matter of the issuance of a preliminary injunction shall be set down for a hearing at the earliest possible time and shall take precedence of all matters except older matters of the same character; and when the same comes up for hearing the party obtaining the temporary restraining order shall proceed with the application for a preliminary injunction, and if he does not do so the court shall dissolve the temporary restraining order. Upon two days' notice to the party obtaining such temporary restraining order the opposite party may appear and move the dissolution or modification of the order, and in that event the court or judge shall proceed to hear and determine the motion as expeditiously as the ends of justice may require.

Section two hundred and sixty-three of an Act entitled "An Act to codify, revise, and amend the laws relating to the judiciary," approved March third, nineteen hundred and eleven, is hereby repealed.

Nothing in this section contained shall be deemed to alter, repeal, or amend section two hundred and sixty-six of an Act entitled "An Act to codify, revise, and amend the laws relating to the judiciary," approved March third, nineteen hundred and eleven.

Sec. 18. Except as otherwise provided in section 16 of this Act, no restraining order or interlocutory order of injunction shall issue, except upon the giving of security by the applicant in such sum as the court or judge may deem proper, conditioned upon the payment of such costs and damages as may be incurred or suffered by any party who may be found to have been wrongfully enjoined or restrained thereby.

Sec. 19. Every order of injunction or restraining order shall set forth the reasons for the issuance of the same, shall be specific in terms, and shall describe in reasonable detail, and not by reference to the bill of complaint or other document, the act or acts sought to be restrained, and shall be binding only upon the parties to the suit, their officers, agents, servants, employees, and attorneys, or those in active concert or participating with them, and who shall, by personal service or otherwise, have received actual notice of the same.

Sec. 20. No restraining order or injunction shall be granted by any court of the United States, or a judge or the judges thereof, in any case between an employer and employees, or between employers and employees, or between employees, or between persons employed and persons seeking employment, involving, or growing out of, a dispute concerning terms or conditions of employment, unless necessary to prevent irreparable injury to property, or to a property right, of the party making the application, for which injury there is no adequate remedy at law, and such property or property right must be described with particularity in the application, which must be in writing and sworn to by the applicant or by his agent or attorney.

And no such restraining order or injunction shall prohibit any person or persons, whether singly or in concert, from terminating any relation of employment, or from ceasing to perform any work or labor, or from recommending, advising, or persuading others by peaceful means so to do; or from attending at any place where any such person or persons may lawfully be, for the purpose of peacefully obtaining or communicating information, or from peacefully persuading any person to work or to abstain from working; or from ceasing to patronize or to employ any party to such dispute, or from recommending, advising, or persuading others by peaceful and lawful means so to do; or from paying or giving to, or withholding from, any person engaged in such dispute, any strike benefits or other moneys or things of value; or from peaceably assembling in a lawful manner, and for lawful purposes; or from doing any act or thing which might lawfully be done in the absence of such dispute by any party thereto; nor shall any of the acts specified in this paragraph be considered or held to be violations of any law of the United States.

Sec. 21. Any person who shall willfully disobey any lawful writ, process, order, rule, decree, or command of any district court of the United States or any court of the District of Columbia by doing any act or thing therein, or thereby forbidden to be done by him, if the act or thing so done by him be of such character as to constitute also a criminal offense under any statute of the United States, or under the laws of any State in which the act was committed, shall be proceeded against for his said contempt as hereinafter provided.

Sec. 22. Whenever it shall be made to appear to any district court or judge thereof, or to any judge therein sitting, by the return of a proper officer on lawful process, or upon the affidavit of some credible person, or by information filed by any district attorney, that there is reasonable ground to believe that any person has been guilty of such contempt, the court or judge thereof, or any judge therein sitting, may issue a rule requiring the said person so charged to show cause upon a day certain why he should not be punished therefor, which rule, together with a copy of the affidavit or information, shall be served upon the person charged, with sufficient promptness to enable him to prepare for and make return to the order at the time fixed therein. If upon or by such return, in the judgment of the court, the alleged contempt be not sufficiently purged, a trial shall be directed at a time and place fixed by the court: *Provided, however*, That if the accused, being a natural person, fail or refuse to make return to the rule to show cause, an attachment may issue against his person to compel an answer, and in case of his continued failure or refusal, or if for any reason it be impracticable to dispose of the matter on the return day, he may be required to give reasonable bail for his attendance at the trial and his submission to the final judgment of the court. Where the accused is a body corporate, an attachment for the sequestration of its property may be issued upon like refusal or failure to answer.

In all cases within the purview of this Act such trial may be by the court, or, upon demand of the accused, by a jury; in which latter event the court may impanel a jury from the jurors then in attendance, or the court or the judge thereof in chambers may cause a sufficient number of jurors to be selected and summoned, as provided by law, to attend at the time and place of trial, at which time a jury shall be selected and impaneled as upon a trial for misdemeanor; and such trial shall conform, as near as may be, to the practice in criminal cases prosecuted by indictment or upon information.

If the accused be found guilty, judgment shall be entered accordingly, prescribing the punishment, either by fine or imprisonment, or both, in the discretion of the court. Such fine shall be paid to the United States or to the complainant or other party injured by the act constituting the contempt, or may, where more than one is so damaged, be divided or apportioned among them as the court may direct, but in no case shall the fine to be paid to the United States exceed, in case the accused is a natural person, the sum of $1,000, nor shall such imprisonment exceed the term of six months: *Provided*, That in any case the court or a judge thereof may, for good cause shown, by affidavit or proof taken in open court or before such judge and filed with the papers in the case, dispense with the rule to show cause, and may issue an attachment for the arrest of the person charged with contempt; in which event such person, when arrested, shall be brought before such court or a judge thereof without unnecessary delay and shall be admitted to bail in a reasonable penalty for his appearance to answer to the charge or for trial for the contempt; and thereafter the proceedings shall be the same as provided herein in case the rule had issued in the first instance.

Sec. 23. The evidence taken upon the trial of any persons so accused may be preserved by bill of exceptions, and any judgment of conviction may be reviewed upon writ of error in all respects as now provided by law in criminal cases, and may be affirmed, reversed, or modified as justice may require. Upon the granting of such writ of error, execution of judgment shall be stayed, and the accused, if thereby sentenced to imprisonment, shall be admitted to bail in such reasonable sum as may be required by the court, or by any justice, or any judge of any district court of the United States or any court of the District of Columbia.

Sec. 24. Nothing herein contained shall be construed to relate to contempts committed in the presence of the court, or so near thereto as to obstruct the administration of justice, nor to contempts committed in disobedience of any lawful writ, process, order, rule, decree, or command entered in any suit or action brought or prosecuted in the name of, or on behalf of, the United States, but the same, and all other cases of contempt not specifically embraced within section twenty-one of this Act, may be punished in conformity to the usages at law and in equity now prevailing.

Sec. 25. No proceeding for contempt shall be instituted against any person unless begun within one year from the date of the act complained of; nor shall any such proceeding be a bar to any criminal prosecution for the same act or acts; but nothing herein contained shall affect any proceedings in contempt pending at the time of the passage of this Act.

Sec. 26. If any clause, sentence, paragraph, or part of this Act shall, for any reason, be adjudged by any court of competent jurisdiction to be invalid, such judgment shall not affect, impair, or invalidate the remainder thereof, but shall be confined in its operation to the clause, sentence, paragraph, or part thereof directly involved in the controversy in which such judgment shall have been rendered.

III. Trade Commission Act

Approved September 26, 1914, Chap. 203

An Act to create a Federal Trade Commission, to define its powers and duties, and for other purposes

Sec. 1. A commission is hereby created and established, to be known as the Federal Trade Commission (hereinafter referred to as the commission), which shall be composed of five commissioners, who shall be appointed by the President, by and with the advice and consent of the Senate. Not more than three of the commissioners shall be members of the same political party. The first commissioners appointed shall continue in office for terms of three, four, five, six, and seven years, respectively, from the date of the taking effect of this Act, the term of each to be designated by the President, but their successors shall be appointed for terms of seven years, except that any person chosen to fill a vacancy shall be appointed only for the unexpired term of the commissioner whom he shall succeed. The commission shall choose a chairman from its own membership. No commissioner shall engage in any other business, vocation, or employment. Any commissioner may be removed by the President for inefficiency, neglect of duty, or malfeasance in office. A vacancy in the commission shall not impair the right of the remaining commissioners to exercise all the powers of the commission.

The commission shall have an official seal, which shall be judicially noticed.

SEC. 2. Each commissioner shall receive a salary of $10,000 a year, payable in the same manner as the salaries of the judges of the courts of the United States. The commission shall appoint a secretary, who shall receive a salary of $5,000 a year, payable in like manner, and it shall have authority to employ and fix the compensation of such attorneys, special experts, examiners, clerks, and other employees as it may from time to time find necessary for the proper performance of its duties and as may be from time to time appropriated for by Congress.

With the exception of the secretary, a clerk to each commissioner, the attorneys, and such special experts and examiners as the commission may from time to time find necessary for the conduct of its work, all employees of the commission shall be a part of the classified civil service, and shall enter the service under such rules and regulations as may be prescribed by the commission and by the Civil Service Commission.

All of the expenses of the commission, including all necessary expenses for transportation incurred by the commissioners or by their employees under their orders, in making any investigation, or upon official business in any other places than in the city of Washington, shall be allowed and paid on the presentation of itemized vouchers therefor approved by the commission.

Until otherwise provided by law, the commission may rent suitable offices for its use.

The Auditor for the State and Other Departments shall receive and examine all accounts of expenditures of the commission.

SEC. 3. Upon the organization of the commission and election of its chairman, the Bureau of Corporations and the offices of Commissioner and Deputy Commissioner of Corporations shall cease to exist; and all pending investigations and proceedings of the Bureau of Corporations shall be continued by the commission.

All clerks and employees of the said bureau shall be transferred to and become clerks and employees of the commission at their present grades and salaries. All records, papers, and property of the said bureau shall become records, papers, and property of the commission, and all unexpended funds and appropriations for the use and maintenance of the said bureau, including any allotment already made to it by the Secretary of Commerce from the contingent appropriation for the Department of Commerce for the fiscal year nineteen hundred and fifteen, or from the departmental printing fund for the fiscal year nineteen hundred and fifteen, shall become funds and appropriations available to be expended by the commission in the exercise of the powers, authority, and duties conferred on it by this Act.

The principal office of the commission shall be in the city of Washington, but it may meet and exercise all its powers at any other place. The commission may, by one or more of its members, or by such examiners as it may designate, prosecute any inquiry necessary to its duties in any part of the United States.

Sec. 4. The words defined in this section shall have the following meaning when found in this Act, to wit:

" Commerce " means commerce among the several States or with foreign nations, or in any Territory of the United States or in the District of Columbia, or between any such Territory and another, or between any such Territory and any State or foreign nation, or between the District of Columbia and any State or Territory or foreign nation.

" Corporation " means any company or association incorporated or unincorporated, which is organized to carry on business for profit and has shares of capital or capital stock, and any company or association, incorporated or unincorporated, without shares of capital or capital stock, except partnerships, which is organized to carry on business for its own profit or that of its members.

" Documentary evidence " means all documents, papers, and correspondence in existence at and after the passage of this Act.

" Acts to regulate commerce " means the Act entitled " An Act to regulate commerce," approved February fourteenth, eighteen hundred and eighty-seven, and all Acts amendatory thereof and supplementary thereto.

" Anti-trust acts " means the Act entitled " An Act to protect trade and commerce against unlawful restraints and monopolies," approved July second, eighteen hundred and ninety; also the sections seventy-three to seventy-seven, inclusive, of an Act entitled "An Act to reduce taxation, to provide revenue for the Government, and for other purposes," approved August twenty-seventh, eighteen hundred and ninety-four; and also the Act entitled "An Act to amend sections seventy-three and seventy-six of the Act of August twenty-seventh, eighteen hundred and ninety-four, entitled 'An Act to reduce taxation, to provide revenue for the Government, and for other purposes,'" approved February twelfth, nineteen hundred and thirteen.

Sec. 5. Unfair methods of competition in commerce are hereby declared unlawful.

The commission is hereby empowered and directed to prevent persons, partnerships, or corporations, except banks, and common carriers subject to the Acts to regulate commerce, from using unfair methods of competition in commerce.

Whenever the commission shall have reason to believe that any such person, partnership, or corporation has been or is using any unfair method of competition in commerce, and if it shall appear to the commission that a proceeding by it in respect thereof would be to the interest of the public, it shall issue and serve upon such person, partnership, or corporation a complaint stating its charges in that respect, and containing a notice of a hearing upon a day and at a place therein fixed at least thirty days after the service of said complaint. The person, partnership, or corporation so complained of shall have the right to appear at the place and time so fixed and show cause why an order should not be entered by the commission requiring such person, partnership, or corporation to cease and desist from the violation of the law so charged in said complaint. Any person, partnership, or corporation may make application, and upon good cause shown may be allowed by the commission, to intervene and appear in said proceeding by counsel or in person. The testimony in any such proceeding shall be reduced to writing and filed in the office of the commission. If upon such hearing the commission shall be of the opinion that the method of competition in question is prohibited by this Act, it shall make a report in writing in which it shall state its findings as to the facts, and shall issue and cause to be served on such person, partnership, or corporation an order requiring such person, partnership, or corporation to cease and desist from using such method of competition. Until a transcript of the record in such hearing shall have been filed in a circuit court of appeals of the United States, as hereinafter provided, the commission may at any time, upon such notice and in such manner as it shall deem proper, modify or set aside, in whole or in part, any report or any order made or issued by it under this section.

If such person, partnership, or corporation fails or neglects to obey such order of the commission while the same is in effect, the commission may apply to the circuit court of appeals of the United States, within any circuit where the method of competition in question was used or where such person, partnership, or corporation resides or carries on business, for the enforcement of its order, and shall certify and file with its application a transcript of the entire record in the proceeding, including all the testimony taken and the report and order of the commission. Upon such filing of the application and transcript the court shall cause notice thereof to be served upon such person, partnership, or corporation and thereupon shall have jurisdiction of the proceeding and of the question determined therein, and shall have power to make and enter upon the pleadings, testimony, and proceedings set forth in such transcript a decree affirming, modifying, or setting aside the order of the commission. The findings of the commission as to the facts, if supported by testimony, shall be conclusive. If either party shall apply to the court for leave to adduce additional evidence, and shall show to the satisfaction of the court that such additional evidence is material and that there were reasonable grounds for the failure to adduce such evidence in the proceeding before the commission, the court may order such additional evidence to be taken before the commission and to be adduced upon the hearing in such manner and upon such terms and conditions as to the court may seem proper. The commission may modify its findings as to the facts, or make new findings, by reason of the additional evidence so taken, and it shall file such modified or new findings, which, if supported by testimony, shall be conclusive, and its recommendation, if any, for the modification or setting aside of its original order, with the return of such additional evidence. The judgment and decree of the court shall be final, except that the same shall be subject to review by the Supreme Court upon certiorari as provided in section two hundred and forty of the Judicial Code.

Any party required by such order of the commission to cease and desist from using such method of competition may obtain a review of such order in said circuit court of appeals by filing in the court a written petition praying that the order of the commission be set aside. A copy of such petition shall be forthwith served upon the commission, and thereupon the commission forthwith shall certify and file in the court a transcript of the record as hereinbefore provided. Upon the filing of the transcript the court shall have the same jurisdiction to affirm, set aside, or modify the order of the commission as in the case of an application by the commission for the enforcement of its order, and the findings of the commission as to the facts, if supported by testimony, shall in like manner be conclusive.

The jurisdiction of the circuit court of appeals of the United States to enforce, set aside, or modify orders of the commission shall be exclusive.

Such proceedings in the circuit court of appeals shall be given precedence over other cases pending therein, and shall be in every way expedited. No order of the commission or judgment of the court to enforce the same shall in any wise relieve or absolve any person, partnership, or corporation from any liability under the antitrust acts.

Complaints, orders, and other processes of the commission under this section may be served by any one duly authorized by the commission, either (*a*) by delivering a copy thereof to the person to be served, or to a member of the partnership to be served, or to the president, secretary, or other executive officer or a director of the corporation to be served; or (*b*) by leaving a copy thereof at the principal office or place of business of such person, partnership, or corporation; or (*c*) by registering and mailing a copy thereof addressed to such person, partnership, or corporation at his or its principal office or place of business. The verified return by the person so serving said complaint, order, or other process setting forth the manner of said service shall be proof of the same, and the return post-office receipt for said complaint, order, or other process registered and mailed as aforesaid shall be proof of the service of the same.

Sec. 6. The commission shall also have power —

(*a*) To gather and compile information concerning, and to investigate from time to time the organization, business, conduct, practices, and management of any corporation engaged in commerce, excepting banks and common carriers subject to the Act to regulate commerce, and its relation to other corporations and to individuals, associations, and partnerships.

(*b*) To require, by general or special orders, corporations engaged in commerce, excepting banks, and common carriers subject to the Act to regulate commerce, or any class of them, or any of them, respectively, to file with the commission in such form as the commission may prescribe annual or special, or both annual and special, reports or answers in writing to specific questions, furnishing to the commission such information as it may require as to the organization, business, conduct, practices, management, and relation to other corporations, partnerships, and individuals of the respective corporations filing such reports or answers in writing. Such reports and answers shall be made under oath, or otherwise, as the commission may prescribe, and shall be filed with the commission within such reasonable period as the commission may prescribe, unless additional time be granted in any case by the commission.

(*c*) Whenever a final decree has been entered against any defendant corporation in any suit brought by the United States to prevent and restrain any violation of the anti-trust Acts, to make investigation, upon its own initiative, of the manner in which the decree has been or is being carried out, and upon the application of the Attorney-General it shall be its duty to make such investigation. It shall transmit to the Attorney-General a report embodying its findings and recommendations as a result of any such investigation, and the report shall be made public in the discretion of the commission.

(*d*) Upon the direction of the President or either House of Congress to investigate and report the facts relating to any alleged violations of the anti-trust Acts by any corporation.

(*e*) Upon the application of the Attorney-General to investigate and make recommendations for the readjustment of the business of any corporation alleged to be violating the anti-trust Acts in order that the corporation may thereafter maintain its organization, management, and conduct of business in accordance with law.

(*f*) To make public from time to time such portions of the information obtained by it hereunder, except trade secrets and names of customers, as it shall deem expedient in the public interest; and to make annual and special reports to the Congress and to submit therewith recommendations for additional legislation; and to provide for the publication of its reports and decisions in such form and manner as may be best adapted for public information and use.

(*g*) From time to time to classify corporations and to make rules and regulations for the purpose of carrying out the provisions of this Act.

(*h*) To investigate, from time to time, trade conditions in and with foreign countries where associations, combinations, or practices of manufacturers, merchants, or traders, or other conditions, may affect the foreign trade of the United States, and to report to Congress thereon, with such recommendations as it deems advisable.

SEC. 7. In any suit in equity brought by or under the direction of the Attorney-General as provided in the anti-trust Acts, the court may, upon the conclusion of the testimony therein, if it shall be then of opinion that the complainant is entitled to relief, refer said suit to the commission, as a master in chancery, to ascertain and report an appropriate form of decree therein. The commission shall proceed upon such notice to the parties and under such rules of procedure as the court may prescribe, and upon the coming in of such report such exceptions may be filed and such proceedings had in relation thereto as upon the report of a master in other equity causes, but the court may adopt or reject such report, in whole or in part, and enter such decree as the nature of the case may in its judgment require.

SEC. 8. The several departments and bureaus of the Government when directed by the President shall furnish the commission, upon its request, all records, papers, and information in their possession relating to any corporation subject to any of the provisions of this Act, and shall detail from time to time such officials and employees to the commission as he may direct.

SEC. 9. For the purposes of this Act the commission, or its duly authorized agent or agents, shall at all reasonable times have access to, for the purpose of examination, and the right to copy any documentary evidence of any corporation being investigated or proceeded against; and the commission shall have power to require by subpoena the attendance and testimony of witnesses and the production of all such documentary evidence relating to any matter under investigation. Any member of the commission may sign subpoenas, and members and examiners of the commission may administer oaths and affirmations, examine witnesses, and receive evidence.

Such attendance of witnesses, and the production of such documentary evidence, may be required from any place in the United States, at any designated place of hearing. And in case of disobedience to a subpoena the commission may invoke the aid of any court of the United States in requiring the attendance and testimony of witnesses and the production of documentary evidence.

Any of the district courts of the United States within the jurisdiction of which such inquiry is carried on may, in case of contumacy or refusal to obey a subpoena issued to any corporation or other person, issue an order requiring such corporation or other person to appear before the commission, or to produce documentary evidence if so ordered, or to give evidence touching the matter in question; and any failure to obey such order of the court may be punished by such court as a contempt thereof.

Upon the application of the Attorney-General of the United States, at the request of the commission, the district courts of the United

States shall have jurisdiction to issue writs of mandamus commanding any person or corporation to comply with the provisions of this Act or any order of the commission made in pursuance thereof.

The commission may order testimony to be taken by deposition in any proceeding or investigation pending under this Act at any stage of such proceeding or investigation. Such depositions may be taken before any person designated by the commission and having power to administer oaths. Such testimony shall be reduced to writing by the person taking the deposition, or under his direction, and shall then be subscribed by the deponent. Any person may be compelled to appear and depose and to produce documentary evidence in the same manner as witnesses may be compelled to appear and testify and produce documentary evidence before the commission as hereinbefore provided.

Witnesses summoned before the commission shall be paid the same fees and mileage that are paid witnesses in the courts of the United States, and witnesses whose depositions are taken and the persons taking the same shall severally be entitled to the same fees as are paid for like services in the courts of the United States.

No person shall be excused from attending and testifying or from producing documentary evidence before the commission or in obedience to the subpoena of the commission on the ground or for the reason that the testimony or evidence, documentary or otherwise, required of him may tend to criminate him or subject him to a penalty or forfeiture. But no natural person shall be prosecuted or subjected to any penalty or forfeiture for or on account of any transaction, matter, or thing concerning which he may testify, or produce evidence, documentary or otherwise, before the commission in obedience to a subpoena issued by it: *Provided*, That no natural person so testifying shall be exempt from prosecution and punishment for perjury committed in so testifying.

SEC. 10. Any person who shall neglect or refuse to attend and testify, or to answer any lawful inquiry, or to produce documentary evidence, if in his power to do so, in obedience to the subpoena or lawful requirement of the commission, shall be guilty of an offense and upon conviction thereof by a court of competent jurisdiction shall be punished by a fine of not less than $1,000 nor more than $5,000, or by imprisonment for not more than one year, or by both such fine and imprisonment.

Any person who shall willfully make, or cause to be made, any false entry or statement of fact in any report required to be made under this Act, or who shall willfully make, or cause to be made, any false entry in any account, record, or memorandum kept by any corporation subject to this Act, or who shall willfully neglect or fail to make, or to cause to be made, full, true, and correct entries in such accounts, records, or memoranda of all facts and transactions appertaining to the business of such corporation, or who shall willfully remove out of the jurisdiction of the United States, or willfully mutilate, alter, or by any other means falsify any documentary evidence of such corporation, or who shall willfully refuse to submit to the commission or to any of its authorized agents, for the purpose of inspection and taking copies, any documentary evidence of such corporation in his possession or within his control, shall be deemed guilty of an offense against the United States, and shall be subject, upon conviction in any court of the United States of competent jurisdiction, to a fine of not less than $1,000 nor more than $5,000, or to imprisonment for a term of not more than three years, or to both such fine and imprisonment.

If any corporation required by this Act to file any annual or special report shall fail so to do within the time fixed by the commission for filing the same, and such failure shall continue for thirty days after notice of such default, the corporation shall forfeit to the United States the sum of $100 for each and every day of the continuance of such failure, which forfeiture shall be payable into the Treasury of the United States, and shall be recoverable in a civil suit in the name of the United States brought in the district where the corporation has its principal office or in any district in which it shall do business. It shall be the duty of the various district attorneys, under the direction of the Attorney-General of the United States, to prosecute for the recovery of forfeitures. The costs and expenses of such prosecution shall be paid out of the appropriation for the expenses of the courts of the United States.

Any officer or employee of the commission who shall make public any information obtained by the commission without its authority, unless directed by a court, shall be deemed guilty of a misdemeanor, and, upon conviction thereof, shall be punished by a fine not exceeding $5,000, or by imprisonment not exceeding one year, or by fine and imprisonment, in the discretion of the court.

Sec. 11. Nothing contained in this Act shall be construed to prevent or interfere with the enforcement of the provisions of the anti-trust Acts or the Acts to regulate commerce, nor shall anything contained in the Act be construed to alter, modify, or repeal the said anti-trust Acts or the Acts to regulate commerce or any part or parts thereof.

IV. Combinations in Import Trade

Act of August 27, 1894, Chap. 349 (Wilson tariff act) as amended by Act of February 12, 1913, Chap. 40

Sec. 73. Every combination, conspiracy, trust, agreement, or contract is hereby declared to be contrary to public policy, illegal and void when the same is made by or between two or more persons or corporations either of whom, as agent or principal, is engaged in importing any article from any foreign country into the United States, and when such combination, conspiracy, trust, agreement, or contract is intended to operate in restraint of lawful trade, or free competition in lawful trade or commerce, or to increase the market price in any part of the United States of any article or articles imported or intended to be imported into the United States, or of any manufacture into which such imported article enters or is intended to enter. Every person who is or shall hereafter be engaged in the importation of goods or any commodity from any foreign country in violation of this section of this Act, or who shall combine or conspire with another to violate the same, is guilty of a misdemeanor, and on conviction thereof in any court of the United States, such person shall be fined in a sum not less than one hundred dollars and not exceeding five thousand dollars, and shall be further punished by imprisonment, in the discretion of the court, for a term not less than three months nor exceeding twelve months.

Sec. 74. The several [circuit courts] [1] of the United States are hereby invested with jurisdiction to prevent and restrain violations of section seventy-three of this Act; and it shall be the duty of the several district attorneys of the United States, in their respective districts, under the direction of the Attorney-General to institute proceedings in equity to prevent and restrain such violations. Such proceedings may be by way of petitions setting forth the case and praying that such violations shall be enjoined or otherwise prohibited. When the parties complained of shall have been duly notified of such petition, the court shall proceed, as soon as may be, to the hearing and determination of the case; and pending such petition and before final decree, the court may at any time make such temporary restraining order or prohibition as shall be deemed just in the premises.

Sec. 75. Whenever it shall appear to the court before which any proceeding under the seventy-fourth section of this Act may be

[1] See note, page 116.

pending, that the ends of justice require that other parties should be brought before the court, the court may cause them to be summoned, whether they reside in the district in which the court is held or not; and subpoenas to that end may be served in any district by the marshal thereof.

SEC. 76. Any property owned under any contract or by any combination, or pursuant to any conspiracy, and being the subject thereof, mentioned in section seventy-three of this Act, imported into and being within the United States, or being in the course of transportation from one State to another, or to or from a Territory or the District of Columbia, shall be forfeited to the United States, and may be seized and condemned by like proceedings as those provided by law for the forfeiture, seizure, and condemnation of property imported into the United States contrary to law.

SEC. 77. Any person who shall be injured in his business or property by any other person or corporation by reason of anything forbidden or declared to be unlawful by this Act may sue therefor in any [circuit court] [1] of the United States in the district in which the defendant resides or is found, without respect to the amount in controversy, and shall recover threefold the damages by him sustained, and the costs of suit, including a reasonable attorney's fee.

(28 Statutes at Large, 570; 37 Statutes at Large, 667.)

V. USE OF THE PANAMA CANAL

Act of August 24, 1913, Chap. 390 (Panama Canal Act)

SEC. 11. No vessel permitted to engage in the coastwise or foreign trade of the United States shall be permitted to enter or pass through said canal if such ship is owned, chartered, operated, or controlled by any person or company which is doing business in violation of the provisions of the Act of Congress approved July second, eighteen hundred and ninety, entitled "An Act to protect trade and commerce against unlawful restraints and monopolies," or the provisions of section seventy-three to seventy-seven, both inclusive, of an Act approved August twenty-seventh, eighteen hundred and ninety-four, entitled "An Act to reduce taxation, to provide revenue for the Government, and for other purposes," or the provisions of any other Act of Congress amending or supplementing the said act of July second, eighteen hundred and ninety, commonly known as the Sherman Anti-trust Act, and amendments thereto, or said sections of the Act of August twenty-seventh,

[1] See note, page 116.

eighteen hundred and ninety-four. The question of fact may be determined by the judgment of any court of the United States of competent jurisdiction, in any cause pending before it to which the owners or operators of such ship are parties. Suit may be brought by any shipper or by the Attorney-General of the United States. (37 Statutes at Large, 567.)

VI. Expedition of Proceedings

Act of February 11, 1903, Chap. 544, as amended by
Act of June 25, 1910, Chap. 428

Sec. 1. In any suit in equity pending or hereafter brought in any [circuit court] [1] of the United States under the Act entitled "An Act to protect trade and commerce against unlawful restraints and monopolies," approved July second, eighteen hundred and ninety, "An Act to regulate commerce," approved February fourth, eighteen hundred and eighty-seven, or any other Acts having a like purpose that hereafter may be enacted, wherein the United States is complainant, the Attorney-General may file with the clerk of such court a certificate that, in his opinion, the case is of general public importance, a copy of which shall be immediately furnished by such clerk to each of the [circuit] [1] judges of the circuit in which the case is pending. Thereupon such case shall be given precedence over others and in every way expedited, and be assigned for hearing at the earliest practicable day, before not less than three of the circuit judges of said circuit, if there be three or more; and if there be not more than two circuit judges, then before them and such district judge as they may select; or, in case the full court shall not at any time be made up by reason of the necessary absence or disqualification of one or more of the said circuit judges, the Justice of the Supreme Court assigned to that circuit, or the other circuit judge or judges may designate a district judge or judges within the circuit who shall be competent to sit in said court at the hearing of said suit. In the event the judges sitting in such case shall be equally divided in opinion as to the decision or disposition of said cause, or in the event that a majority of said judges shall be unable to agree upon the judgment, order, or decree finally disposing of said case in said court which should be entered in said cause, then they shall immediately certify that fact to the Chief Justice of the United States, who shall at once designate and appoint some circuit judge to sit with said judges and to assist in determining said cause.

[1] See note, page 116.

Such order of the Chief Justice shall be immediately transmitted to the clerk of the circuit court in which said cause is pending, and shall be entered upon the minutes of said court. Thereupon said cause shall at once be set down for reargument and the parties thereto notified in writing by the clerk of said court of the action of the court and the date fixed for the reargument thereof. The provisions of this section shall apply to all causes and proceedings in all courts now pending, or which may hereafter be brought.

SEC. 2. In every suit in equity pending or hereafter brought in any [circuit court][1] of the United States under any of said Acts, wherein the United States is complainant, including cases submitted but not yet decided, an appeal from the final decree of the circuit court will lie only to the Supreme Court and must be taken within sixty days from the entry thereof: *Provided*, That in any case where an appeal may have been taken from the final decree of a circuit court to the circuit court of appeals before this Act takes effect, the case shall proceed to a final decree therein, and an appeal may be taken from such decree to the Supreme Court in the manner now provided by law. (32 Statutes at Large, 823; 36 Statutes at Large, 854.)

VII. WITNESSES AND TESTIMONY

Act of February 25, 1903, Chap. 755 (Legislative, Executive and Judicial Appropriation Act for the fiscal year 1904)

SEC. 1. . . . For the enforcement of the provisions of the Act entitled " An Act to regulate commerce," approved February fourth, eighteen hundred and eighty-seven, and all Acts amendatory thereof or supplemental thereto, and of the Act entitled " An Act to protect trade and commerce against unlawful restraints and monopolies," approved July second, eighteen hundred and ninety, and all Acts amendatory thereof or supplemental thereto, and sections seventy-three, seventy-four, seventy-five, and seventy-six, of the Act entitled " An Act to reduce taxation, to provide revenue for the government, and other purposes," approved August twenty-seventh, eighteen hundred and ninety-four, the sum of five hundred thousand dollars, to be immediately available, is hereby appropriated, out of any money in the treasury not heretofore appropriated, to be expended under the direction of the Attorney-General in the employment of special counsel and agents of the Department of Justice to conduct proceedings, suits and prosecutions under said Acts in the courts of the United States:

[1] See note, page 116.

Provided, That no person shall be prosecuted or be subjected to any penalty or forfeiture for or on account of any transaction, matter, or thing concerning which he may testify or produce evidence, documentary or otherwise, in any proceeding, suit or prosecution under said Acts:

Provided further, That no person so testifying shall be exempt from prosecution or punishment for perjury committed in so testifying. (32 Statutes at Large, 904.)

Act of June 30, 1906, Chap. 3920

Under the immunity provisions in the Act entitled " An Act in relation to testimony before the Interstate Commerce Commission," and so forth, approved February eleventh, eighteen hundred and ninety-three, in section six of the Act entitled " An Act to establish the Department of Commerce and Labor," approved February fourteenth, nineteen hundred and three, and in the Act entitled " An Act to further regulate commerce with foreign nations and among the States," approved February nineteenth, nineteen hundred and three, and in the Act entitled " An Act making appropriations for the legislative, executive, and judicial expenses of the Government for the fiscal year ending June thirtieth, nineteen hundred and four, and for other purposes," approved February twenty-fifth, nineteen hundred and three, immunity shall extend only to a natural person who, in obedience to a subpoena, gives testimony under oath or produces evidence, documentary or otherwise, under oath.

(34 Statutes at Large, 798.)

Act of March 3, 1913, Chap. 114

An Act Providing for Publicity in Taking Evidence under the Act of July second, eighteen hundred and ninety

In the taking of depositions of witnesses for use in any suit in equity brought by the United States under the Act entitled " An Act to protect trade and commerce against unlawful restraints and monopolies," approved July second, eighteen hundred and ninety, and in the hearings before any examiner or special master appointed to take testimony therein, the proceedings shall be open to the public as freely as are trials in open court; and no order excluding the public from attendance on any such proceedings shall be valid or enforceable. (37 Statutes at Large, 731.)